MESSY INCARNATION

MEDITATIONS ON CHRIST IN PROCESS

BRUCE EPPERLY

Energion Publications
Gonzalez, Florida
2022

ISBN: 978-1-63199-822-5
eISBN: 978-1-63199-823-2
Library of Congress Control Number: 2022945568

Energion Publications
PO Box 841
Gonzalez, FL 32560

https://energion.com
pubs@energion.com

TABLE OF CONTENTS

With gratitude to my teachers – Richard Keady, Marie Fox, John Cobb, David Griffin, and Bernard Loomer – who made process theology come alive for me and the congregations and institutions where I have shared the good news of process theology as professor, pastor, and chaplain – Central Michigan University, Georgetown University, Wesley Theological Seminary, Lancaster Theological Seminary, Christian Theological Seminary, Claremont School of Theology and South Congregational Church, United Church of Christ, Centerville, Massachusetts. I am grateful to my companions in the "Messy Incarnation: Jesus in the Twenty-first Century" class, held on zoom through South Congregational Church during a time of pandemic, July to September 2020, and involving participants from across the country. Ubuntu, "I am because of you."

PROLOGUE

WONDER AND WORRY

In 1975, my first year as a theology student at Claremont Graduate School in California, John Cobb's *Christ in a Pluralistic Age* was published. Cobb's book transformed my theological vision and way of life. To a fledging process theologian, Cobb in person and in print articulated a living Christology in which the creative spirit of Christ could be found in art, everyday life, science, the world's faith traditions, architecture, and the non-human world. All-embracing in impact and inspiration, Christ is the source of creative transformation in the movements of ecology, literature, liberation, and political protest as well as in the worship and theological traditions of the church. As a result of Cobb's insights, I came to believe that the Word made flesh in Jesus of Nazareth transforms societies as well as spirits when we embrace its embodied presence in our personal and corporate lives.

Cobb's Christological reflections have stood the test of time. Cobb anticipated many of the changes we are currently facing in society and congregational life. If anything, over the past five decades, social and spiritual change has accelerated. Change has become the norm in spirituality, theology, society, and politics. Though many want to hold onto the past, the old order in politics, demographics, and religion is passing and an uncertain and fragile new order is emerging. Institutional Christianity has been pushed to the margins with the fastest-growing North American spiritual movements occurring among those who describe themselves as "none of the above" and "spiritual but not religious."

The face of North American Christianity is global and multicultural, not just European. Once religious transformation moved at a glacial pace, but now the polar ice caps of tradition are collapsing at breakneck speed and old certainties regarding doctrine, authority, and truth are being swept away like the sands of my familiar Cape Cod beaches.

Seismic shifts in culture occur with increasing rapidity and the unthinkable has become normal in North American religion and politics: those who once claimed to be the moral and doctrinal police and defenders of orthodoxy now march in lockstep with political leaders known for their infidelity, dishonesty, bullying, racism, and pandering to dictators and racists. Those who once claimed an inside track on doctrinal and biblical absolutes are now promoting moral relativism and alternate facts to achieve political and cultural goals. Conservative Christians are among the most ardent purveyors of easily-refuted conspiracy theories. Fearful of losing their place in society, many conservative Christians have cultivated a crusade, and ironically also a victim, mentality assuming God is on their side and that those who hold contrasting viewpoints threaten *their* marriages, ability to practice *their* religion, and, frankly, in many cases, *their* white privilege. In their conflation of religion and public policy, politics has supplanted faith in God as their ultimate concern. Many self-proclaimed orthodox Christians appear to have sold their souls for a Supreme Court justice, the repeal of Roe versus Wade, and the maintenance of the old order of white heterosexual privilege.

The growing culture wars and social changes were only exacerbated during the 2020 pandemic election year, when the USA political leadership was unable to respond with either effectiveness or empathy to the Coronavirus pandemic or the Black Lives Matter protests. Christians became leaders in denying medical science along with climate change and promulgating unfounded conspiracy theories. Wearing masks and practicing safe distancing became a matter of politics and faith perspective rather than prudence and compassion. Claiming the right of their congregations to do what they please without governmental restrictions, the question "what would Jesus do?" was supplanted by "don't tread on me" as Christian zealots risked their neighbors' wellbeing for the convenience of not wearing a mask, worshipping in enclosed spaces, and going to tightly packed campaign rallies. This crisis of faith has been brewing since the emergence of the Moral Majority in the 1970s and will continue its reactive quest for political control in the face of growing ethnic, racial, and spiritual pluralism. We can expect more of this in the future as the old religious order, now under siege by social and religious change, will fight to the death to maintain its white Christian privilege. Following the election, many conservative Christian leaders and their followers seemed more intent to preach the gospel of a rigged election than proclaim the life-changing faith of Jesus Christ. Despite a new presidential administration in the United States, we will continue to deal with issues of racism, incivility, environmental destruction, and the quest among conservative Christians to turn back the clock to a time when minorities and non-Christians knew their place and protest was an anomaly.

To persons beyond the silos of Christendom, the compassionate and welcoming Jesus, whose circle of love embraced humanity in its wondrous diversity and whose prophetic critiques focused on the machinations of the wealthy, powerful, and religiously orthodox, has been eclipsed by scorched earth politics, the condemnation of opponents as evil, heretical, and unpatriotic, alignments with oligarchs and billionaires, and silencing prophets of planetary well-being. Christianity's complicity with racism, homophobia, climate denial, and economic injustice has been starkly revealed in the deaths of George Floyd and others, scapegoating of the LGBTQ community, and the response to America's original sins of racism and First Nations genocide on theological as well as party lines.

If Christendom isn't already dead, the most prominent cheerleaders of orthodoxy are killing it as a spiritual option for millennials and emerging generations who view Christianity as anti-science, anti-LGBTQ, anti-environment, anti-immigrant, anti-woman, anti-intellectual, anti-immigrant, anti-Muslim, anti-racial equality, and now anti-fact, anti-medicine, anti-science, and anti-safety. Christianity has already lost traction among baby boomers for whom the New York *Times* and Starbucks are perceived as more spiritually edifying than Sunday morning worship. In the eyes of millions of North Americans, the Christian exceptionalism touted by conservative Christianity and the racism reflected in hate crimes and the incarceration of toddlers are fabricated from the same ideological cloth. The most vocal politically conservative Christians have found their contemporary Constantine and defenders of the "true" faith in authoritarian politicians, whose most draconian policies are identified with Christian orthodoxy and whose words, even prevarications, are honored as if they come from the Second Person of the Trinity. When John Shelby Spong asserted that "Christianity must change or die," he had no idea that the greatest threat to Jesus' message would not be outmoded theological positions but the polarizing rhetoric of those who claim to be most theologically orthodox. Yet, Spong's insights still ring true: bad theology, grounded in authoritarian images of God and doctrine absolutism, leads to dangerous economic, governmental, environmental, and public policy. The orthodox Christian response to the pandemic – often characterized by risky behavior and science denial - has further accelerated suspicion of Christianity among millennials and younger persons as well as their college-educated elders.

While the decidedly unchristian marriage of religion, sexuality, race, guns, and politics has made headline news, those of us who claim to represent the progressive wing of Christianity have been pushed further and further to the margins. Apart from the brief attention given to the Poor Peoples Campaign, over the past decade and during this era of protest and pandemic, progressive Christianity has been virtually unnoticed by the media and overlooked by young adults, both of which fix their attention and animus on the vitriolic rantings and hypocrisy of televangelists and Bible-toting politicians and assume that because we share the label "Christian," we are cut from the same ideological and political fabric. Only occasionally does our message of an inclusive, earth and science-affirming, prophetic and socially just Christianity receive attention from journalists and politicians.

In times of social and cultural crisis, we need to reclaim the way of Jesus the Christ, the first-century Jewish healer, and savior, whose revelation embraces, inspires, and affirms every life-supporting cultural and wisdom tradition. Despite the rise, and likely fall, of twenty-first-century Constantinian Christianity and its Trump-Church, there is a glimmer of hope that Jesus' radically inclusive and transformational message can be recovered and that the margins of progressive theology and spirituality become the frontiers of adventurous faith. Inspired by Jesus rather than Caesar, the spiritual desert may bloom again, and progressive Christianity may burst forth with a vital, life-changing, open-spirited, and life-transforming personal and planetary message. The heart of this message will be a renewed emphasis on Jesus as healer, prophet, earth lover, and spiritual companion and our role as Jesus' companions in fostering these earth and person-affirming values.

WHEN CRISIS BECOMES OPPORTUNITY

For many of us who have dedicated our lives to theological and congregational leadership, the survival of the progressive movement in Christianity, like the survival of the planet as we know it, is in doubt. To survive, Christianity, even our own progressive visions of faith, must die to self-interest and binary thinking and awaken to world loyalty. Ironically, our survival as a viable movement means letting go of security and opening to creativity. We must be open to creative transformation in the interplay of God's call and our response. This is especially true in our time of pluralism, protest, and pandemic in which deep down we know that things will never ever be the same again for the institutions we cherish and upon whose fidelity we depend.

Openness to the way of Jesus, which joins treasuring the past and moving forward toward God's future, involves holding our worry about the future in contrast with wonder at this amazing universe and beautiful planet and the calling that has been placed before us to claim our role as God's companions in healing the earth. Gratitude, grace, and glory for the wonders of God's love embodied in earth, sky, and sea, and creation in its amazing diversity will inspire and undergird our doctrinal message and prophetic politics.

It's all about time, that is, the concrete moment in history, and immersing ourselves in the messiness and uncertainty of our time and discovering that our time is the right time, the "Kairos" moment when we align ourselves with Jesus' vision of Shalom and transformation. The progressive faith of the future will not hold onto the past but take chances on God's visions for the future. Then, again, isn't this the message of Jesus – those who lose their lives will find them, and those who try to hold onto their lives and place in the social order will lose them? Isn't this the message of the prophets who called the wealthy to economic sacrifice so they can once again experience God's vision for their lives?

It may come as a surprise but most of the Bible was written in times of crisis when the future of the tribe, community, nation, or movement was in doubt!

Our survival as a progressive movement is intimately related to the larger issue of planetary survival and for this, we need a miracle. Not a supernatural act of a sleeping and apathetic deity awakened by our prayers, but the miracle of creative transformation that comes when we claim our identity as Jesus' companions in healing the world, inspired and enlivened by God's energy of love flowing through us. As June Jordan says in her poem to the South African women, we must recognize that we don't need to wait for others, right now in this uncertain moment "we are the ones we have been waiting for."[1] We are the spiritual children of the kenotic Christ, who immerses himself in our world to bring healing and wholeness to the least of these and hope for transformation to those

---

1   June Jordan, "Poem for South African Women", written in
     commemoration of the 40,000 women and children who protested on
     August 9, 1956 against the policy requiring all black Africans over sixteen
     years old to carry pass books. Presented at the United Nations on August
     9, 1978.

in privilege and power. (Philippians 2:5-11) We are the ones whose movement from privilege to prayer and apathy to empathy prepares the way for unleashing God's power to save the world.

IT'S ALL ABOUT JESUS

One summer morning as I was taking my sunrise walk on a Cape Cod beach, a disheveled man shouted "It's all about Jesus" as he rode along on his bicycle. In many ways, despite his roughhewn and idiosyncratic demeanor, his words rang true. That same day, my wife Kate observed that I seldom invoke explicitly Jesus' name in worship or preaching but focus primarily on God the Creator and Companion. Like many progressives, I confess that while Jesus the Christ is always present in my thinking, my preaching and prayers tend to be theologically inclusive and God-centered. My language focuses more on the Creative Wisdom whose power and presence move throughout the universe and our personal lives than doctrinal statements about the first-century Galilean prophet and healer whose Spirit still moves in our world.

Many progressives, like myself, believe our focus on God implicitly means speaking of Jesus and his presence in the world. Focusing primarily on the Galilean Jesus seems too narrow, too exclusionary, in an age of plural spiritual paths. The vision of a cosmic Christ fits our theological and spiritual universalism more comfortably than a Galilean prophet. And, yet God's revelation is always historical and concrete, and salvation is always local as well as global.

In this pivotal moment of Christian and global history, indeed, it may be "all about Jesus." God inspires Jesus and Jesus reveals God. Jesus shapes our concrete and intimate experiences as well as the global arc of history. Proclaiming Jesus does not detract from our affirmation of pluralism. Following the way of the Galilean teacher inspires a spiritually centered pluralism, grounded in faithfulness to Jesus' all-embracing vision of Shalom.

The heart of the Christian message is that the Infinite is also Intimate. And, theologically speaking, that Infinite-Intimate presence has often been described as Jesus the Christ. God is present in the face of every newborn, most particularly in the birth of the Christ Child in the Bethlehem stable. The presence of God in Bethlehem and Jerusalem radiates across our planet, guiding, inspiring, and transforming. As the historically embodied revelation of God's vision of Shalom, justice, and healing, personally and globally, Jesus manifests the second-century theologian Iranaeus' affirmation: the glory of God is a human being fully alive.

The heart of the incarnation, the Word and Wisdom of God made flesh in the messiness of our world, is God's full immersion in our lives, not as wholly other and apathetic, but as fully human, one of us, celebrating and suffering in the tragic beauty of our lives. The fully human one, often seen as cognate with the "Son of Man," is Jesus of Nazareth whose full humanity enables the fullness of God to come alive in our world. In opening to Jesus' way, we experience amazing grace that saves our lives and enables us to flourish despite "many dangers, toils, and snares." In following Jesus, we become fully alive to the joy and pain of the world. In embracing Jesus' way, we embody his challenge to authoritarian, binary, exclusivist images of God and ecclesiastical power.

In reclaiming a personal relationship with Jesus, and the evangelical spirit of my youth, I am rediscovering God's presence addressing me in the messy and complicated challenges of my own life as pastor, professor, parent and grandparent, citizen, and privileged North American. I am discovering that the One who "walks with me and talks with me and tells me I am his own" also addresses everyone else with the same loving intimacy, often disguised in our personal and political lives and present as a catalyst in every quest for personal and planetary healing. I am discovering that I can affirm my own "Jesus-y" faith, to quote Anne Lamott, and recognize Jesus' companions in every quest for truth and healing, whether in a Buddhist meditation group, Sufi dance, protest on the borderlands or at the nation's capital, Black Lives Matter peaceful protest, or a Friday student climate strike. Wherever there are healing and transformation of body, mind, spirit, and relationships, I find Jesus present, not seeking glory like a politician in need of the roar of the crowd, but moving in our cells and souls, often anonymously to bring abundant life to all God's creation. The living Jesus is infinitely personal and flexible and fully bound to time and space along with his rootedness in the everlasting God. Jesus reflects and mirrors the deepest needs and the most creative possibilities of ours and every time.

To follow Jesus today joins personal faith and salvation with planetary and social well-being. Indeed, Jesus' vision of salvation, as wholeness, always inspires the quest for healing in the wondrous messiness and temporality of our personal and communal lives. In an interdependent universe, the personal and planetary are one and the healing of the planet nurtures my spirit and my own healing contributes to healing the earth. The Living Christ, embodied in Jesus of Nazareth, reconciles all things and guides us in our quest to companion God in the healing of creation, human and non-human alike. The healer of Nazareth embodies and shows us the far horizon of personal, relational, and planetary wholeness.

As I seek to reclaim the Personal Jesus along with the Cosmic Christ, I am inspired by the image of the Celtic cross, the traditional upright cross reinforced by a circle where the two horizontal and vertical planks join. I see Jesus' presence in the lure of the moral and spiritual arc of history, patiently moving through the conflicts and joys of the world and our lives, relentlessly calling us toward God's vision of Shalom. I also see Jesus in the circular movements of the seasons, in summer and winter, and seedtime and harvest, which join order and novelty, as well as tradition and transformation. In Jesus Christ, we discover that the ever-changing and ever-faithful meet.

My vision of the Celtic cross inspires me to seek the living Jesus in the repetitive stories found in the seasons of the Christian year, meditating on Jesus' life and mission and our response to it in terms of the yearly cycle of Advent, Christmas, Epiphany, Lent, Holy Week, Easter, Pentecost, Creation Season, and the Realm of Christ. Comforting in their yearly familiarity, these seasons also reflect God's mercies, which are new every morning and inspire us to discover Jesus' presence in the novelties and threats of our own time. Following Jesus means telling the "old, old story" in new and creative ways and embodying Jesus' mission in ways his first followers could not have imagined.

The One who is the same yesterday, today, and tomorrow, moving through the cycles of nature and the Christian year, is also the One who provides fresh possibilities for this unique and challenging moment in our lives and history. Jesus as the Incarnation of divine love and wisdom inspires the dynamic and evolving moral and spiritual arcs of history. Accordingly, as I seek to share a vision of Jesus the Christ, grounded in the insights of process theology and progressive Christianity, I will look at Jesus' life and mission through the lens of the seasons of the Christian year, earth-based and divinely guided, hoping to deepen my relationship with Personal Jesus and Cosmic Christ as inspirations for us to claim our vocation as God's companions in healing the earth. In joining the forward arc of history with the circularity of divine dependability, we discover that we are Jesus' contemporaries and companions. The first and twenty-first centuries merge as we discover Jesus' real presence in the challenges, sufferings, and joys of our time.

I don't claim to describe the fullness of Christ in my reflections on the seasons of Christian experience. Jesus will always remain a mystery, and like the Holy Spirit, freely moving and not constrained by our doctrines and institutions. Still, these seasons, I believe, provide glimpses of God's messy incarnation in the lives of persons and nations and the earth which supports our existence, in our lives right now!

Spiritual transformation – what Paul describes as having the mind of Christ - will not come through fanfare, theocracy, bible-thumping, proof-texting, or bloviation, nor will it come through a renewal of Constantinian political and military crusades against presumed infidels. It will be inspired and renewed through embodied and historical movements of call and response. Spiritual transformation emerges through God's call, our response, and God's response to our call, persistent, adventurous, and open-spirited in our embrace of the energy of love still present and evolving in the humble, life-transforming Healer from Galilee.

A WORD ON METHOD AND MEANING

My meditations on messy incarnation, experiencing Jesus the Christ in the joyful and tragic world in which we live, join both first and twenty-first centuries. As a theologian, spiritual guide, and pastor, not to mention a humble believer whose faith integrates mysticism, evangelical piety, intellectual acuity, and social and planetary concern, I take seriously the many streams of Jesus scholarship. I have found wisdom from scholars as diverse as Marcus Borg, N.T. Wright, John Dominic Crossan, Ben Witherington, Obery Hendricks, Howard Thurman, Cynthia Bourgeault, Richard Horsley, and Burton Mack. I recognize that Jesus will always be a mystery, transcending our intellectual and literary studies. Our understanding of Jesus must be faithful to the scriptures and the most inspirational of the non-canonical gospels (such as Thomas and Mary of Magdalene), but we must recognize the "real" Jesus cannot be confined to the text and that our understanding of Jesus always mirrors our social and theological location.

The first-century Jesus is evolving, both in our understanding and in terms of Jesus the Christ's influence and presence in the world. The facts of his life as we can dimly intuit them, are constantly being reimagined. The ecumenical creeds of the first few centuries of Christianity are the beginning and not the end of our theological and spiritual journeys. Just as he was in the first century, Jesus is always a contemporary, speaking to us the word we need to hear to embrace God's vision of Shalom in our time and place. The first-century gospel writers and those who told the stories of Jesus were inspired by God and their relationship with Jesus, and so are we. Their stories are grounded on the bedrock of personal experience, and so are ours. Their accounts of Jesus are finite and shaped by their faith, and so are ours. Jesus' first followers as well as those who told stories and then constructed the gospels experienced Jesus as a healer who changed bodies as well as spirits and social location, a prophet who challenged social and religious injustice, a visionary imagining an alternative reality of Shalom, a storyteller, mystic, spiritual guide, and one whose message transcends death.

Their accounts were not fabricated but reflected lived experiences of personal and community transformation. Sermonic in nature, they are "true" even if particular events are not always "factual." They remind us that our twenty-first-century rationalism often constricts rather than liberates our understanding of the universe. The world, God, and ourselves are more amazing than we can ever imagine – all trillion galaxies – and may reflect a "deeper magic," as C.S. Lewis avers in *The Lion, The Witch, and The Wardrobe,* an amazing energy of love that makes a way beyond what we can currently imagine, not in violating the patterns of nature but as their fullest realization.

Christ is always in process! As was the case with the two pilgrims on the path to Emmaus, Jesus is known in the walking and the eating, the journey and community.

Jesus lives on! Christ is alive in the push and pull of history and the challenges of our personal lives. Jesus will be found in the walking and praying and seeing our own personal and global pilgrimage through the experiences of the Fully Human One who walked the highways and byways of Judea. In the spirit of God's open-ended inspiration, let us begin our journey with Jesus in the spirit of the Indian folk tune I learned in the Baptist church of my youth, committing ourselves to being Jesus' companions in our messy, troubled, and beautiful world.

I have decided to follow Jesus;
I have decided to follow Jesus;
I have decided to follow Jesus;
No turning back, no turning back.

The world behind me, the cross before me;
The world behind me, the cross before me;
The world behind me, the cross before me;
No turning back, no turning back.

CHAPTER TWO

ADVENT: A WAY
WHERE THERE IS
NO WAY

O ne of my favorite songs from the rock musical "Godspell" is "Prepare Ye." At the sound of John the Baptist's cry to "prepare," a motley group of people walking along crowded city streets throw off their shoes and coats, joyfully frolic in an urban pool, pouring water over each other's heads in sacramental response, and leaving their jobs behind to join in the God's coming realm of Shalom. Once aimless, they now find purpose and a way forward. Once alone, they now have become a beloved community. Once imprisoned by social convention, now they dance and sing. Baptized by grace, they come alive. They don't fully know the One they are following. They don't even know where they're going. But the way of Jesus will be known in the walking and dancing.

It is commonplace to assume a quantum leap in spiritual maturity and faith between Jesus' family and first followers and ourselves. We believe that we live in different worlds spiritually as well as historically. We assume that Jesus' first female and male disciples, not to mention his parents Mary and Joseph, and his relatives Elizabeth and Zechariah, had a level of certainty and obedience that we lack.

The Gospels tell a far different story. Mary, Joseph, and Zechariah struggle with their role as agents of messianic incarnation. The Gospels describe the disciples as a contentious, fickle, and impatient cadre, often ignorant of their leader's intentions and mission, who nevertheless followed their teacher with all their doubts and imperfections. As they began the journey with Jesus, setting forth in an uncertain religious and political context, I suspect that Jesus' first followers, like the characters from "Godspell" and us, felt like

Dag Hammarskjold, United Nations General Secretary from 1953-1961. Written on Pentecost, just a few months before his death, Hammarskjold confessed:

> I don't know Who – or what – put the question. I don't know when it was put. I don't even remember answering. But at some moment I did answer *Yes* to Someone – or something – and from that hour I was certain that existence is meaningful and, that, therefore, my life, in self-surrender, had a goal. From that moment I have known what it means "not to look back" and "to take no thought for the morrow."[2]

In saying "yes" to the Way of Jesus, God who had always been in their lives awakened them to their calling as God's beloved children and companions in changing the world. In embracing Jesus, they became little Christs themselves! God is still calling fallible humans. God is calling us, sometimes softly and tenderly, other times fiercely and majestically. Not fully aware of what following Jesus will mean for us – or cost us – we venture forth as did Jesus' first followers.

Advent is the season of faithful agnosticism and hopeful adventuring in which Jesus and his mission become known to us on the journey. Advent is the season of divine restlessness and impatience with the way things are in our lives and in the world. In Advent, we look toward the coming of the child who will change everything and the Savior whose vision is far over the horizon challenging every value system, institutional mission statement, and national policy.

We can't stay put because God won't stay put. God's discontentment with the injustice of the status quo pushes us out into the highways and byways with the good news that life can be different, the nation can be transformed, the powerful can care, and our political leaders can be driven to their knees in prayerful obedience God's way and not the devices and desires of their hearts. Advent pushes us into the chaotic maelstrom and messiness of time and

---

2   Dag Hammarsjold, *Markings* (New York: Knopf), 1964 p. 169.

space – the expectation of a Messiah in the first century and the hope of survival in our time. The future is in doubt, the old order is crumbling, and yet a light emerges on the far horizon.

The Christ of Advent is on the move, globally and personally, doing a new thing, imagining a new world, and inspiring people to join the adventure. Not yet born in the so-called first century – most scholars date Jesus' birth in the vicinity of 4 BCE -or embodied in our twenty-first-century world, Jesus invites, lures, and challenges us toward the far horizons of morality and spirituality. The impulses that gave birth to the universe and spun forth galaxies beyond number move through our lives toward horizons of hope despite the recalcitrance of history. Inspired by God's energy of love, Advent proclaims a deeply incarnational way of life that beckons us to continually embark on pilgrimages of the Spirit, trusting God's movements in our lives and history, never fully knowing the destination or whether success will attend our journeys. Like the Celtic spiritual guides of an earlier era, we set out on the high seas of spiritual adventure and justice-seeking on our equivalent of small boats, called coracles, often without map or rudder, trusting that God will guide our boat to our personal "place of resurrection," the spot where we will discover God's birth among us and embody God's message with our unique set of gifts and life experiences. The sea is great, and our boat is so small. The problems appear unsolvable and our resources meager. Yet the One who walked upon the water guides wind and wave and the quest for Shalom in our time. In walking with him, we can face the storms with resources beyond our imagination.

ADVENTUROUS ADVENT

Advent is the season of adventure, risk, and suspense. Though the future is in doubt, the One who calls us forward to be companions in mission will venture forth with us, providing us with visions and the energy to embody them in the quest for Shalom.

Advent, in its restless complexity, is the season of preparation and pregnancy, reminding us that Jesus is born in the fullness of time – the Kairos season - as the fulfillment of the moral and spiritual arc of history proclaimed by Israel's prophets. Embedded in the complexities of history, God comes to us concretely in a first-century child. Jesus' birth occurs in the historical, cultural, ethnic, and political maelstrom of first-century Judea. When history is most desperate, a voice emerges from the wilderness, calling for personal and political transformation. A teacher and healer arises, awakening our souls to a world yet to be born. The people who walked in darkness have seen a great light. Those who lack hope for the future discover a pathway through the conflicts and complexities of history. New hope emerges in response to our current hopelessness. A way is made when we perceive no way forward.

The prophetic restlessness of Advent is inspired by God's vision of Shalom. The child to be born is the heir to the prophetic imagination of alternative realities to the injustices and false Messiahs that populate history. The divine pathos, as Abraham Joshua Heschel asserts, describes the prophetic vision of a God who has skin in the game, who mourns children separated from their parents on the USA borderlands, grieves the violent deaths of African American fathers at the hands of the police, and rebukes nations who willfully destroy the earth for short term profits. Prophets then and now share God's anger at poverty, injustice, and violence toward the vulnerable. Our spiritual restlessness mirrors God's own restlessness, calling us beyond the false gods of nationalism, consumerism, and the rallies of celebrity politicians, to embody the vision of a new heaven and new earth, where our sons and daughters will learn the ways of peace, the streets will fill with laughter and celebration, and no child go without food, water, education, or housing.

Quantum leaps of possibility, emerging out of the darkness of conflict and despair, lure us forward, offering images of hope and the energy to embody the hopes we affirm. Yet, although Jewish history prepared for and found its zenith in the birth and ministry of Jesus, the moral and spiritual arc of history incarnate in Jesus has not reached its goal. In the twenty-first century, we are still waiting for the apocalypse, the revealing, of global and personal healing. The realm of God is "now" – among us and within us – but "not yet" – not fully realized just as we have not become fully alive to God's vision for us and our society. Our world is still in process, pushing toward visions of wholeness amid personal and planetary threats. We are restless for creative transformation, and our quest for beauty inspires us to create institutions that heal the earth and its peoples.

THE ZECHARIAH MOMENT

Not yet born, Jesus is the driving force in Advent theology and spirituality. When our son was young, we gave him an Advent calendar. Each day he was greeted with a scripture passage and a chocolate. In the spirit of Forrest Gump's mother's wisdom, each morning brought a new flavor, some sweet and others bittersweet. He never knew what he was going to get and that was part of the fun! Like that childhood calendar, Advent is both surprising and bittersweet. Those who received the message of the coming Messiah first-hand were shocked, surprised, and pushed beyond their comfort zones. They were amazed and afraid.

The Advent stories, rooted in the prophetic history of Judaism and the hope for the peaceable realm, enlighten our own contemporary histories. God comes to us in our own history and we are amazed and afraid. The Jesus we encounter, whose vision is still not fully born in the first and twenty-first-century Advents, is not an exception to the historical process and the quest for justice but the fulfillment of prophetic history and our own personal and political quests. Jesus' birth and ministry are not part of a divinely ordained and predestined rescue operation taking us beyond the ambiguities of history. Instead, the coming Child invites us to embody God's vision on earth as it is in heaven. The realm of God is among us, embodied in the hoped-for Messiah and our hope for God's realm to be born in us and our world. Good news abounds in flesh and blood – of a little child in Bethlehem, in our cells and souls, in our struggles to find meaning, and in the birth of all God's children. The providential arc of history aims toward beauty, justice, and transformation. God's arc of history is proclaimed by prophets and way makers: "Repent, turn around, and choose a new route, you powerful and privileged ones." The world is going to be turned upside down, the poor will flourish, and the wealthy left empty-handed, the powerless promoted and the powerful demoted, proclaims Mary of Nazareth. Mary's relative by marriage Zechariah receives good news and a surprising vocation that will change the lives of Elizabeth and himself as well as the planet.

We are Zechariah. We come to worship. We fulfill our professional callings, not expecting anything surprising or spectacular but like Isaiah, who retreated to the Jerusalem Temple in a time of national crisis, we may encounter the Holy One and discover our calling is much greater than we imagined. (see Isaiah 6:1-8)

Faithful to God, the childless Zechariah does his duty as a Temple priest. He plans on performing the prescribed rituals he has done throughout his professional career. He expects to serve God in prayer and then return to Elizabeth and the quiet of their home. Without warning, an angel appears in the inner sanctum, turning Zechariah's world upside down.

> Now at the time of the incense offering, the whole assembly of the people was praying outside. Then there appeared to him an angel of the Lord, standing at the right side of the altar of incense. When Zechariah saw him, he was terrified; and fear overwhelmed him. But the angel said to him, "Do not be afraid, Zechariah, for your prayer has been heard. Your wife Elizabeth will bear you a son, and you will name him John. You will have joy and gladness, and many will rejoice at his birth, for he will be great in the sight of the Lord. He must never drink wine or strong drink; even before his birth he will be filled with the Holy Spirit. He will turn many of the people of Israel to the Lord their God. With the spirit and power of Elijah he will go before him, to turn the hearts of parents to their children, and the disobedient to the wisdom of the righteous, to make ready a people prepared for the

Lord." Zechariah said to the angel, "How will I know that this is so? For I am an old man, and my wife is getting on in years." The angel replied, "I am Gabriel. I stand in the presence of God, and I have been sent to speak to you and to bring you this good news." (Luke 1:9-19)

The good news of creative transformation and messianic incarnation can be terrifying. The fulfillment of what we have prayed for is often more than we can ask or imagine. Answers to prayer, whether the birth of a child or a new social order, turn everything upside down. We may with Zechariah become mute with wonder. In the Zechariah moment, the personal meets the planetary. The realization of his personal hope, the birth of a child, is part of a much larger story, the dream of the new age of Shalom. He is frightened and so are we as we ponder Advent and the coming of God's realm, not as a binary divine rescue operation separating the saved and unsaved but as a process in which we have a role that will require forsaking familiar habits, going against the grain, standing apart from the crowd, and sacrificing our comfort, largesse, and reputation for a greater good. To the consternation of his community, Zechariah goes against custom, naming the child "John" rather than his own name or that of a relative.

Zechariah and Elizabeth come to realize that their hopes are part of a Greater Hopefulness and that their son, leaping joyfully in utero at the presence of the prenatal Jesus and his mother, will be the harbinger of God's new age.

And you, child, will be called the prophet of the Most High;
  for you will go before the Lord to prepare his ways,
to give knowledge of salvation to his people
  by the forgiveness of their sins.
By the tender mercy of our God,
  the dawn from on high will break upon us,
to give light to those who sit in darkness
    and in the shadow of death,
  to guide our feet into the way of peace. (Luke 1:76-79)

EMBRACING THE WILDNESS OF DIVINE POSSIBILITY

Advent is about provocative and life-changing possibilities that invite us to imagine ourselves and the world in new ways. The world is chockful of divine inspiration. Every moment can be a theophany, bearing divine witness, when we cleanse the doors of perception and say "yes" to God's holy adventure.

With Mary, we respond "How can this be?" as we hear angelic voices of hope. Like Mary, we respond, not fully knowing the cost of our response, "with God all things are possible," but coming to realize that we must be the mothers and midwives of the Holy Birth in our time.

Later that same bold Mary recognizes that her child will turn everything upside down. The Advent hope revolutionizes persons and political structures, balancing the scale between the powerful and powerless, and wealthy and impoverished.

> My soul magnifies the Lord,
>   and my spirit rejoices in God my Savior,
>   for he has looked with favor on the lowliness of his servant.
>   Surely, from now on all generations will call me blessed;
>   for the Mighty One has done great things for me,
>   and holy is his name.
> His mercy is for those who fear him
>   from generation to generation.
> He has shown strength with his arm;
>   he has scattered the proud in the thoughts of their hearts.
>
> He has brought down the powerful from their thrones,
>   and lifted up the lowly;
> he has filled the hungry with good things,
>   and sent the rich away empty.
> He has helped his servant Israel,
>   in remembrance of his mercy,
> according to the promise he made to our ancestors,
>   to Abraham and to his descendants forever.
> (Luke 1:46-55)

The prenatal Jesus lures us toward a transvaluation of values. Mary's hymn is both personal and political. In fact, our individual spiritual and our political values can't be separated in incarnational theology. The impossible possibility of God's vision of Shalom is at hand, and it still is at hand, challenging us to become the change we want to see in the world as we seek as God's prophetic companions to topple the unjust structures of our time.

PROPHETIC POSSIBILITY

In the spirit of the Hebraic prophets and Jesus' first followers, we feel the birth pangs of new creation in our cells and souls. The dreams of prophets inspire and empower us. And yet death remains. Death on the city streets and death from the Coronavirus. The rich and powerful still prefer darkness to light in their willingness to sacrifice hundreds of thousands of lives for economic gain and brutalize protestors to maintain their thinly viewed racist illusion of law and order. The powers and principalities prosper, and the earth is destroyed by human greed. Our own national leaders, drunk on wealth, power, and self-interest, muffle the cries of prophets to seek their own personal profit. They abandon unborn generations of human children along with the non-human world by denying the signs of the times in Australian and Western USA forest fires, collapsing icebergs, species edging toward extinction, and carbon dioxide at the 350 parts per million tipping point. With hope in short supply as we view 24/7 cable news, we need a vision of a new world order, the beloved community, the peaceable realm, in which the lion and the lamb lie down together, children play safely, and weapons of war give way to agricultural implements.

This future will not be realized by the fake news of constantly updated predictions of the Second Coming and their impact on USA Middle East policy, but by love of the earth and its peoples and the realization that although God's vision will outlive our planet, the very DNA of God is embedded in our world through the birth of a child and God will not abandon God's beloved world. We need an Advent spirituality, a theology of hopeful realism, and we need it now, to inspire our commitment to be God's companions in healing the earth.

Advent plunges us into the complex realities of Jesus' history and our own. Jesus is incomprehensible apart from the prophets, wisdom sages, matriarchs, patriarchs, and political leaders of Israel. Their DNA courses through his body, mind, and spirit. Their struggles inspire his mission. The spiritual child of Hebraic prophets and revolutionaries, not to mention the immigrant Ruth, Jesus lived his entire life in occupied territory. He had no political power or social and economic equity. Judea's own religious leaders were bought and paid for by the oppressing Romans. Visions of hope and feelings of hopelessness characterized the first-century world in which Jesus lived. Many in Jesus' time believed that their only hope was a divine intervention, a catastrophic apocalypse, unilaterally destroying the Roman oppressors and their religious sycophants.

Though many of us have ranged far from the spiritual origins of Jesus' faith, the interplay of hope and hopelessness still shapes our response to the world to which Jesus comes today. Hope is born in the affirmation that we can change ourselves and our nation. Conversely, hopelessness is revealed in our political and economic focus on consumption as ultimate concern.

"Eat, drink, and be merry, for tomorrow we will die" is the unconscious mantra of hopeless consumption and climate change denial. The bumper sticker announcing that "whoever dies with the most toys wins" betrays the meaninglessness that undergirds our consumption. Lost in the universe and led by short-sighted leaders, we focus on the immediate with little concern for future generations, including our own children and grandchildren.

Advent hope, embodied in Mary, Elizabeth, and Zechariah, challenges us to get up off our couches and protest injustice, believing that history still matters and that we are God's hands and feet in securing a more perfect union and more just future. Hope requires an open future and a God who lets go of control as God invites us to be God's own hands, feet, and partners in saving the world.

IMAGING AN ADVENT GOD

We become like the gods in whom we trust. Open-spirited images of God encourage agency, while images of God as all-determining and binary promote self-interest and passivity in terms of our planetary future. Our hopes for historical and social transformation are challenged by the historical hopelessness of adherents to Second Coming theologies of earth destruction and divine abandonment. The faux theology and constantly revised chronology of Jesus' imminent world-destroying return inspires foolhardy visions of apocalyptic catastrophe while stoking climate change denial. Visions of an omnipotent, earth-destroying deity, dampen any concern for environmental well-being, while these same end-times Christians seek rights to parklands and protected places for financial gain! Some apocalyptic soothsayers want to force God's hand, fast-forwarding the Second Coming by their bellicosity in the Middle East.

The words of the Christmas carol are particularly poignant in our time as we yearn for an authentic savior who will change our lives and change our world:

> The hopes and fears
> Of all the years
> Are met in thee tonight.

PREPARING FOR VOCATION

In every moment, in life's messiness, there is a voice singing "prepare ye" and reminding us that there is no Second Coming. Today is the day of salvation. This is the time of our lives and this is the day of salvation. God comes to us in every moment, every firing synapse, every unexpected encounter, and every restless quest for personal and political transformation.

Nearly fifty years ago, John Cobb asked the question, "Is it too late?" in the first text on the theology of ecology. While Cobb did not give a timetable of environmental destruction, we are now in the perfect storm of climate change denial, political upheaval, current and future pandemics, nationalism, and cyber threat that threatens to undermine any global quest to save the earth and its creatures. And, yet, in the spirit of Isaiah, the adventures of teenager Greta Thunberg give us a glimmer of hope that the children and youth of our planet will lead us from darkness to light. While not Messiahs, surely Greta Thunberg, along with the Parkland youth protesting our bloodlust preference of guns over our children, and dare we say following God's way of peace, and Black Lives Matter marchers seeking liberty and justice for all, embody the growing edge of Advent. God's comings will outlast our waywardness, making a way in the wilderness and freshness to parched and hopeless spirits.

Then and now, Messiahs are expected amid what Reinhold Niebuhr describes as the ambiguities of history. Within the hopelessness of history and our despair as we experience our personal helplessness to right the course of our national and planetary life, there is a seed of hope germinating. In the womb of Mary and the womb of our imaginations, life is growing and this life is the light of the world. It will emerge as Jesus' life did, awakening us to God's future, striving for righteousness and love, with no guarantee of success.

In the summer of 1980, my wife and I were living in Tucson, Arizona, and expecting our first child. Up the street from our apartment was a Christian commune, whose leaders had deciphered the end times code, determining that Jesus would come again in July. They quit their jobs and rented cabins in Mount Lemon, presumably to be closer to Jesus when he descended from heaven to earth, rapturing them to the faraway heavens while Tucson would be obliterated. Kate and I lived by another vision of hope, embodied in the growth of our child, quietly and deliberately caring for the unborn child, imagining our future as his parents. A recently minted Ph.D. in a tight job market, I was uncertain where the future would lead us and was worried that we might have to secure our parents' financial support to care for the child. In July 1980, our son Matt was born and is now the parent of two lively boys himself. No world-destroying apocalypse, but a life-giving eschaton, an inspirational future that has guided us for forty years and now inspires us to be companions with God in the quest for justice and earth care. Jesus is here in the birth of a child, not in mountaintop escapes from the conflicts of daily life and political power struggles. Jesus is embodied in the not-yet realized hopes of history not a predetermined rescue operation for a handful of "believers."

Advent is a passionate, restless season in which agnosticism and hope join to pull us forward toward new horizons. We don't always know the way or the contours of God's future, but trust a way will be made through the wilderness, leading us from apathy to empathy and injustice to Shalom. Advent will be known in the walking. The challenges of life will be solved in the seeking. Christ's coming will be experienced moment by moment and day by day in the loving, reorienting our spiritual GPS as the first-century Jesus recalibrated the spirits of the women and men who followed him. As Albert Schweitzer affirmed, no doubt describing his own as well as Jesus' first followers' -and also our own - encounter with the Living Jesus:

> He comes to us as One unknown, without a name, as of old, by the lakeside, He came to those men who knew Him not. He speaks to us the same words: "Follow thou me!" and sets us to the tasks which He has to fulfill for our time. He commands. And to those who obey Him, whether they be wise or simple, He will reveal Himself in the toils, the conflicts, the sufferings which they shall pass through in His fellowship, and, as an ineffable mystery, they shall learn in their own experience Who He is.[3]

The way of Jesus is found in the walking. The God of Restless Empathy revealed in the Advent Jesus, inspires us to move from individualistic apathy and intentional ignorance to share in God's own compassionate empathy and activist awareness. God is revealed in the cries of the poor, in the groanings of creation, and in the restlessness in our own hearts. Jesus grows, a human fetus, one of us, in

---

3   Albert Schweitzer, *The Quest for the Historical Jesus* (London: A&C Black, 1941), 401.

Mary's womb. No supernatural fast-forwarding of pregnancy, but 280 days of growth, fragile, sometimes uncomfortable, the miracle of new life bursting forth in troubled times. The Advent Jesus is the fetus growing in a Palestinian mother, yearning for freedom, and the dream of a Syrian refugee father, hoping against hope to return home. We see the spirit of Advent in environmental activism, social protest, marches for justice and equality, and everyday kindnesses of ordinary people who go beyond their comfort zones to welcome the "other" and who sacrifice from their largesse so that children they will never meet can dream big and achieve greatness.

These are the dreams of the Advent Jesus, who walks beside us on our pilgrim way. Embedded and embodied, God with us, growing in the uncertainties of history, Fully Empathetic, Fully Human, Fully Divine. In all the uncertainties of history, a Child is conceived and grows, inspiring our Advent prayers.

All around us worlds are dying and new worlds are being born;
> All around us life is dying and life is being born.
> The fruit ripens on the tree;
> The roots are silently at work in the darkness of the earth
> Against the time when there shall be new leaves, fresh blossoms, green fruit.
> Such is the growing edge!
> It is the extra breath from the exhausted lung,
> The one more thing when all else has failed,
> The upward reach of life when weariness closes in upon all endeavor.
> This is the basis of hope in moments of despair,
> The incentive to carry on when times are out of joint
> and persons have lost their reason; the source of confidence
> when worlds crash and dreams whiten into ash.
> The birth of a child – life's most dramatic answer to death –
> This is the growing edge incarnate.
> Look well to the growing edge![4]

---

4   Howard Thurman, *The Growing Edge* (Richmond, IN: Friends United Press, 180).

CHAPTER THREE

CHRISTMAS: MESSY INCARNATION

When I was eight years old, I thought Christmas would skip our family that year. Each Christmas of my young life, Santa Claus came to our Salinas Valley home while my brother and I were asleep. When we awakened on Christmas morning, brightly colored packages awaited us beneath a lighted tree. But 1960 would be different. After my father taped his weekly devotional at the local radio station KRKC, we would drive down from our home in King City in the Salinas Valley to Los Angeles to celebrate Christmas with my aunt and uncle. As I pondered the trip south, I wondered, "Will we have any presents this year? How will Santa find us if we're not home on Christmas morning? Can Santa find us if we're not in the usual place?"

When Christmas Eve came, I was anxious as my father dropped our family off at a congregant's home for Christmas treats. After an hour or so of Christmas carols, cookies, and hot chocolate, my father returned and my brother and I were packed into the car. As we headed out of town, my father suddenly exclaimed, "Oh no, I forgot something important. We have to go home to pick it up." As we turned the corner onto our street, my brother and I were startled to see Christmas lights shining and discover presents beneath the brightly lit tree. It was the best Christmas of my childhood. I discovered that even if we were leaving home on Christmas Eve, Santa would find us. Christmas would come regardless of where we were or when we celebrated it. In the night of chaos and uncertainty, God's light shines, showing us the way, where we imagine no way forward.

The Christmas Season is a time of surprise and adventure. A time of great expectation and hope for transformation. When – and where - we don't expect a theophany, God shows up, providing us with more than we can ask or imagine. In our deepest uncertainty, when the future is in doubt, God provides a way forward, making a way where there is no way, creating a highway through the desert, bringing blossoms in an arid land and direction to our aimlessness. God's Wisdom (Logos and Sophia) takes flesh in darkness as well as light, in chaos as well as familiarity, making a way to wholeness where we see only despair. Even when you leave the familiar and change your physical address or even your previous religious belief system, locating yourself in a new religious sphere, God's Word and Wisdom made flesh will find and inspire you.

For most of us, Christmas is truly the loveliest season of the Christian year. The birth of a child, God's response to wayward humankind. A mother's love and a father's protection. The fullness of God in a helpless infant. Divinity among the forgotten. God's innermost being taking birth among our lives, settling down and tenting among us, near as our next breath, fragile as a newborn, deep as parental love, and wide as the imagination can roam. A star on the horizon guides strangers from a strange land, and the light from that same star inspires our adventures into strange and unfamiliar places.

Christmas is the season of Hallmark movies and their affirmation that Christmas is the season of love and miracle, in which anything is possible. The reality of Christmas challenges the Scrooge and Grinch in all of us to expand our hearts to embrace the poor and lonely. Christmas carols awaken us to the reality of "Joy to the world, the Lord is come" in this present moment, in which amid our own personal and national crises, we feel divine empathy and encouragement to face the hopes and fears of all our years.

As I write these words in the Fall of 2020, I yearn for the Christmas spirit. As the song says, "we need a little Christmas." The nation and planet have been turned upside down by the Coronavirus. Protesters march in the streets, rightly challenging four hundred years of racism, as current as an African American male crying out to his deceased mother, "I can't breathe" while being throttled by those meant to protect and serve, or the announcements of indictments relating to a young woman, Breonna Taylor, recklessly shot while sleeping during a police raid. The Coronavirus has kept most of us home, giving the environment a much-needed rest from our willful pollution and reminding us that we need to simplify our lives to ensure the wellbeing of future generations. Yet, despite the impact of the pandemic, political leaders caught up in greed and unable to look beyond economic and political gain roll back environmental protections, fan the flames of racism with code word comments, and deny science to promote their political agenda. There is nothing new in this. Despite our hope in the moral and spiritual arcs of history, it often appears that little has changed since the time of Caesars, Herods, and the world of forced migration and political powerlessness in which the Christ child was born. Yes, "we need a little Christmas" to cheer and liberate our spirits. We also need to experience divine incarnation in the messiness of our personal and political lives. We need an incarnation right now in our world of protest and pandemic as we face our hopes and fears in an increasingly dangerous and complicated world, in which we can discern no clear direction forward.

THE POLITICS OF CHRISTMAS

The Christmas season joins the personal and political. Christmas past at the Bethlehem stable inspires us to empathy and compassion, while we live in the anxieties and threats of Christmas present and like Dicken's Scrooge hope for future Christmases in which political and personal repentance and transformation are possible.

Christmas is also the season of what Alfred North Whitehead describes as tragic beauty. The interplay of beauty and tragedy tells the story of God's revelation in a first-century child born in difficult circumstances with no room at the inn and also in the plight of millions of twenty-first-century children in refugee camps and separated from their families on the USA border, whose pain and powerlessness recapitulates the realities of the first Christmas on a daily basis.

Christmas joins the universal and historical. Rooted in time, the incarnation challenges and confronts political power plays:

> In those days a decree went out from Caesar Augustus that all the world should be registered. (Luke 2:1)
> In the time of King Herod, after Jesus was born in Bethlehem, magi from the East came to Jerusalem. (Matthew 2:1)

The Infinite Wisdom of God is embodied in the rough and tumble world of politics and policing. God's revelation is always historical and contextual. God's vision takes flesh in the realities of economics, political decision-making, and foreign policy as well as personal ethics and spiritual practices. Today, we might speak of Jesus' incarnation as taking place in the "year of the great pandemic," "in the year George Floyd was killed," or "the year of Donald J. Trump's reelection campaign." Jesus' birth comes at the "right time," the "Kairos" moment, in which our hopes and fears meet divine providence and inspiration.

The tragic beauty of Christmas stands out as we consider the political and cultural context of Jesus' birth. Jesus and his parents never lived a day of their lives as free people. They never voted or had a say in their day-to-day political and economic lives. They lived in occupied territory, subject without legal redress to the whims of their Roman occupiers as well as bloodthirsty Jewish surrogates like Herod whose appetite for power and prestige eclipsed their loyalty to their nation. Herod stayed in power through fear and through the machinations of secret police, torture, and state-sponsored violence. A proud people, with a sense of their unique place in history, the Jewish people were reduced to servitude. Augustus' registration of the Roman Empire's peoples was a prelude to taxation without representation, the exacting of tributes to support Roman extravagance, military occupation, and the luxurious lifestyles of treasonous potentates like Herod the Great and his minions.

Though cosmic in impact, divine incarnation takes place among the powerless and put upon. With few resources of their own, Mary and Joseph pilgrim to Joseph's ancestral village where Mary gives birth to the Christ child in a stable because there was no room in the inns of Bethlehem. Without power, privilege, and place of residence, the homeless Christ child is born. The Savior of the World comes without fanfare, another inconsequential Roman subject and mouth to feed, and yet this humble birth is accompanied by tidings of great joy for the lost and lonely, put upon and powerless. Incarnation in a fragile newborn. Everlasting light in a backstreet stable. Divine blessing in a parent's love. Repeated billions of times in world history, and yet each birth reveals something of the Christ child. "The true light, which enlightens everyone, was coming into the world." (John1:9)

ENCOUNTERING INCARNATION

Our hearts are warmed by the Christmas stories. We don't need to fixate on their historical accuracy or the lyrical chronology depicted in our Christmas pageants. Historical deconstructionism and biblical literalism both miss the point. Although textual, historical, sociological, and cultural studies are essential to understanding Jesus and his time, they cannot capture the mystery of divine revelation. The poetry and mysticism of incarnation also defy fundamentalist and literalistic understandings of Jesus' birth. God is always more than we can imagine and the Christ child breaks through every attempt to locate the divine in a church, scripture, ritual, or ideology. The mystery and miracle of incarnation cannot be reduced to words or analyses, for in the humble birth at Bethlehem, the Word and Wisdom of God, is made flesh and the energy that brought forth the big bang is found to be loving energy moving through every cell and soul, luring all creation toward God's Shalom in this moment and beyond history itself.

The Christmas stories in their many dimensions reveal a God who can be touched and a God who touches us. The little baby has skin, and so does God! The Christmas stories reveal our own ambiguous historical adventures for we are the mothers and fathers of the Christ child, the awestruck shepherds, the adventurous magi, and the hard-hearted powerful, and privileged. We are, as participants in God's wondrous incarnation, the little Christs in whom Jesus takes birth in our time and place. We are also the midwives of incarnation in prayers and protests and in mentoring the next generation of little Christs, our children and grandchildren, and children and grandchildren everywhere, who enter this life "trailing clouds of glory" and need our nurture and commitment to fulfill their spiritual destinies.

The Christmas season is about encountering God in ways that transform our lives. The angels of Christmas remind us that inspiration can come to anyone at any time. The Christmas stories are global and universal. They are equally personal, intimately addressing the simple as well as the sophisticated and the poor as well as the privileged. In all its messiness, incarnation challenges us to be people of empathy and imagination.

Imagine Mary! A young woman, dreaming of her future, surprised by an angelic encounter. Unimaginative theological and philosophical minimalists scoff at the possibility of angelic beings and messengers from God, appropriately disguised to respond to our unique personal and historical situations. Yet we cannot determine the scope of reality by our current knowledge or belief. We cannot limit divine creativity, ingenuity, and possibility. A non-coercive God comes to us in diverse and intimate ways that address our personal and cultural experience calling us to become more than we could have previously imagined. In a trillion galaxy universe, guided by an infinitely resourceful divinity, we cannot assume we are the crown of creation. The possibility of gradations of creaturely existence from the angelic to the microcosmic opens us to a variety of incarnational moments. Moreover, an infinitely present and resourceful God can appear in our lives in a variety of ways and personages, providing us with guidance and inspiration, and provocative possibilities, to embody the moral and spiritual arc of evolution.

Yes, imagine Mary, confronted by the angel "Gabriel," with the most amazing possibility, to become God's chosen mother, giving birth to God's chosen messenger for salvation and creative transformation. Mary says "yes" to being the mother of divine revelation, not fully aware of the potential cost to her marriage, reputation, and personal well-being. Was she the first young woman God asked? Could other young women have counted the cost of discipleship and then turned away, changing their lives and the contours of revelation forever?

Mary said "yes," awakening to possibilities beyond her imagination. Awakening to the joys and pain of raising a "special" child. With the exception of Jesus, the fallible and earthy Mary is the supreme biblical manifestation of the ongoing, moment-by-moment "call and response" that characterizes the relationship of God and the world. As the philosopher Alfred North Whitehead asserts:

> God's purpose is always embodied in particular ideals relevant to the actual state of the world ... Every act leaves the world with a deeper or fainter impress of God. He then passes to his next relation to the world with enlarged, or diminished, presentation of ideal values.[5]

While the world lives by the incarnation of God in every moment of experience, there are moments in which we say "yes" to God's great vision, giving birth to God's dreams in unique and life-changing, indeed, world-changing ways.

We don't need to get lost in the mechanics and physiology of Mary's pregnancy. In a world of a trillion galaxies, a virgin birth is possible and not necessarily counter to naturalistic causation. Embedded in our dynamic and energetic universe, there may be a deeper naturalism that evades the unimaginative scholar. Still, traditional and literal understandings of the virgin birth, connected

---

5   Alfred North Whitehead, *Religion in the Making* (New York: Meridian Books, 1972), 152.

with the doctrine of original sin and the inherent sinfulness of sexuality, and Mary's perpetual virginity minimize not only God's revelation to Mary but our own affirmation of our humanity in its fullness. As Irenaeus asserts, the glory of God is a fully alive human and in the moment of saying "yes" to Gabriel, Mary was fully alive and fully open to divine possibility. Her openness has nothing to do with the "immaculate conception," the belief that Mary was born without the taint of original sin, the "virgin birth" or Mary's "perpetual virginity." Sexuality is not a fall from grace or a transmitter of sin, but a loving expression of the love that brought forth the universe and guides our planet's evolutionary process.

Process theology affirms the reality of sin and our distance from God's vision both personally and globally, but equally proclaims the original wholeness of creation. God's Child takes on the wondrous flesh of our beautiful, yet ambiguous world. While sin involves turning from God's vision and clouding our awareness of God's call in our lives, God's quest for human wholeness and planetary healing is never defeated by our waywardness. While we can't affirm "felix culpa," the affirmation of a happy sin that merits such a savior, given the stark realities of human suffering, we can count on God having the resources to make a way where there is no way and to redeem what can be saved in the fallibilities and achievements of humankind and our institutions.

As the scriptures suggest, despite her mystical encounter and unique birthing process, Mary didn't always understand her son Jesus. She herself was finite and limited in understanding despite her deep love for Jesus, and the "queen of heaven" likely enjoyed the human intimacies of sexuality and gave birth to at least six children – in addition to Jesus - according to the normal processes of conception and gestation (Matthew 1:24-25 and Mark 6:3).

What is unique about Jesus' "virgin birth" is that it involved Mary and Jesus! Stories of virgin births were circulated about the divine Caesars and other potentates throughout history. Their military and political greatness were seen to have had their origins in the profound separation from mortals like us. By contrast, God's revelation comes to the vulnerable and powerless, the millions of mothers and children unnoticed by politicians and the media. A young girl without any political and social qualification gives birth to divine possibility whose impact dwarfs that of any self-important sovereign or politician. Mary herself becomes a channel of prophetic wisdom when she responds to another unique pregnancy that of Elizabeth's and the prenatal witness of the one who was to become John the Baptist:

> God has scattered the proud in the thoughts of their hearts.
> He has brought down the powerful from their thrones,
> and lifted up the lowly;
> he has filled the hungry with good things,
> and sent the rich away empty. (Luke 2:51-53)

Mary's holiness emerges in her awakening to God's movements in the lives of fetuses, who will grow up to be agents in God's vision of planetary healing. Humble as Mary is in the social and political order, this powerless woman living in an occupied land embraces God's vision for humankind and gives birth to God's vision of Shalom in the maelstrom of first and twenty-first-century history. As a participant in our zoom seminar exclaimed, "a relatable mother and relatable child reflect a relatable God." Incarnation is about unity and solidarity and not separation and differentiation.

Imagine Joseph! An initially reluctant vehicle of divine revelation, Joseph is not an afterthought in the gospel birth stories. He is front and center in God's birthing in the world of flesh, blood, and politics. Although he comes from what today would be the lower middle class, he still participates in a patriarchal society. Mary's pregnancy threatens his honor and place in the community. Unless he covers it up, and quietly dispatches Mary, he will be the cuckold of the village. Yet, Joseph is a good man, who wants to protect both Mary's life and reputation. Within the concrete political and cultural limitations we face, God provides possibilities for Joseph and for us. God alerts Joseph through a dream to his responsibility in nurturing the unexpected child's embodiment of God's vision of Shalom. Like Mary, Joseph listens to God, despite his misgivings and becomes a channel of divine creative transformation. Attuned to the voice of God and like his Hebraic namesake Joseph of the coat of many colors, whose dreams saved his family, Joseph receives revelatory dreams directing him to flee to Egypt and later to return home when the politics of Judea make it safe for his family to return.

In speaking of Joseph's revelatory dreams, it is essential to remember that Jesus and his family were political refugees. Mary and Joseph crossed the border into Egypt to secure safety for their infant. Like millions today, they risk violence, persecution, and personal safety to leave their familiar homeland to ensure the well-being of their family. Would Jesus have survived apart from the kindness of strangers, most likely within the Jewish community residing in Egypt? Would a contemporary Jesus have been separated from his parents at the USA borders? Perhaps Jesus' own social location along with stories of his family's refugee experiences alerted him to God's presence in the "least of these" and the reality that our treatment of the least of these shapes God's experience of the world.

In the messiness of history, God inspires people today to seek shelter through emigrating to a foreign land. Incarnational theology inspires us to see Jesus and the Holy Family in the faces of immigrants on the USA borderlands and Syrian refugees. Going beyond the European portrait of Jesus and race-related immigration policies, the incarnation reveals divinity in persons of color in search of asylum, whose refugee stories mirror those of the olive-skinned Mary, Joseph, and Jesus.

We cannot read the Christmas story without empathizing with political and economic refugees everywhere. While we need to maintain border integrity and encourage legal immigration, as I write these words in September 2020, the USA is still convicted by the cruel and traumatizing realities of family separation, especially the separation of toddlers and young children from their parents.

You can see young Jesus in every toddler's face, and we can view the scowl of Herod in the heartless visages of national leaders, including our own. You can glimpse shades of Herod in institutional racism and dehumanizing immigration practices that deface the image of God in the least of these.

We cannot talk about the messiness of Christmas without taking note of the massacre of the children, ordered by King Herod. Fearful that he would be supplanted, Herod commands that all young children in the region of Bethlehem would be slaughtered (Matthew 2:16-18). No doubt the One who took the children on his knees and blessed them was painfully aware that his survival was bought at a price. The cries of parents and the fears of children soon to be victims of state-sponsored terrorism may have haunted Mary and Joseph throughout their lives. As the incarnation of Divine Companionship and Compassion, Jesus experienced the cries of suffering children, the grief of parents, and the hard-heartedness of potentates who sacrifice children, either through violence or public policy, for power, prosperity, and political gain.

God is the fellow sufferer who understands and the joyful heart who celebrates. God cries along with the Bethlehem mothers, mourning the slaughter of their children. God experiences the hopelessness of parents separated from their children to fulfill the campaign promises of a self-interested political leader. God feels the terror of a child running for his life in a war-torn land and the panic of an adult on the streets of Minneapolis, Minnesota, crying for mercy, "I can't breathe." God places you on God's knees in prayerful embracing. God never places God's knee on your spiritual neck!

Incarnation is painful. The God with Skin feels our anguish from the inside out and inspires us to seek justice on the behalf of children everywhere.

Imagine Shepherds! Each Christmas I sing "The First Noel" and ponder the lines "on a cold winter night that was so deep." For the first century shepherd, there was no romance to their work. Although shepherds took pride in caring for their flocks and would go out into the wilderness on a dark night to save a lost sheep, as Jesus' parable describes, shepherds were primarily hired hands, working at low salaries, with little social status. Like "essential employees" during the time of the Coronavirus pandemic, their work was risky and often unpleasant. They were considered expendable and were recruited from unskilled and marginalized communities. As a result of the 24/7 nature of their work, the shepherds may also have been religious outsiders, unable to share in the rituals of their faith.

As we read the encounter of the shepherds and angels in our zoom seminar, I heard the story again "for the first time." I read the words about the shepherds "living in the fields." Was their dwelling place restricted to the fields, just getting by from month to month? Did they have homes to go back to? Or were they separated from their families, like many of today's immigrants, so they could support their loved ones with the modest wages they received?

The scandal and beauty of the incarnation is that God's angelic chorus regales the unkempt and smelly and not the elite and powerful of Jerusalem. God detours around Carnegie Hall, the megachurch worship arena, the White House, the political fundraiser, and the gothic cathedral to show up to undocumented field workers, line workers at a meat processing plant, out-of-work machinists and auto workers sporting red MAGA hats, and Jamaican women working at Cape Cod nursing homes.

God loves dirt as well as Lysol. Scuffed shoes as well as wingtips. Worn and calloused hands as well as agile computer fingertips. The aroma of shepherds and farm animals is sweet incense to the newborn Savior. The caring touch of a nursing home aide is as holy to God as the laying on of hands of a televangelist.

The word of God's messengers to Mary, Joseph, the shepherds and those frightened by God's presence and the possibilities that will ensue is "don't be afraid" or as a youth Christmas play in a local Cape Cod church asserted, "Don't freak out!" These words speak to us as God confronts us with impossible possibilities and amazing promises in our own time of hope and hopelessness.

Imagine Magi! At first glance, the Magi appear to be the exception to God's incarnation among the poor and powerless. They are among the privileged and prosperous. They can take a year off to follow a star! Although we will encounter the Magi more fully when we explore the season of Epiphany, the Persian Magi are also outsiders, likely viewed with suspicion when they entered Herod's court with news of a momentous birth. To Herod's court, these foreigners cannot be the chosen recipients of divine revelation because of their Zoroastrian faith tradition and foreign birth. Incredulously, the Jerusalem political and religious elites ask, "Why would God reveal divine wisdom outside the orthodox channels of faith? Why would persons from other faiths have more insight about our faith tradition than we do?"

God's wisdom is unbounded. The reality "in whom we live and move and have our being" inspires Greek poets and philosophers as well as Hebraic prophets and Christian mystics. (Acts 17:28) Magi from a foreign land follow a star to Bethlehem and God is still speaking through the voices of First American spiritual guides, African Yoruba wise ones, Muslim imams, Buddhist monks, Hindu rishis, and the companions of Gandalf and Dumbledore. Don't stifle revelation! When God comes to humankind through a working-class infant from a family struggling to get by to bless the whole earth, every place can be Bethlehem and every child Christlike.

INCARNATION EVERYWHERE

Matthew and Luke give us the kid, while John gives us the cosmos. John's Gospel makes a bold claim for the incarnate Jesus. The Galilean who walked among us is the revelation of God's ever-present and ever-active Wisdom and Word. God's revelation in Jesus born among us touches all creation. God's presence in Jesus is not an anomaly, a divine supernatural rescue operation foreign to flesh and blood, but the energy of love, as primordial as the Big Bang, that brings forth galaxies and planets, evolves flora and fauna, and courses through our cells and souls.

In the beginning was the Word, and the Word was with
God, and the Word was God. He was in the beginning with
God. All things came into being through him, and without him
not one thing came into being. What has come into being in
him was life, and the life was the light of all people. The light
shines in the darkness, and the darkness did not overcome it...
The true light, which enlightens everyone, was coming into the
world. (John 1:1-5, 9)

The intimacy of Bethlehem is also the infinity of divine creativity. God is uniquely revealed in a baby's first cry and the ongoing inspiration to this child growing in wisdom and stature. (Luke 2:52) Within the spiritual history of the Jewish people, and the mystical experiences of patriarchs, matriarchs, and prophets, God chose certain moments to be particularly present and definitive of history. Just as there are certain definitive and revelatory moments in our lives, there are definitive and revelatory moments in God's relationship with humankind. Surely the incarnation was one such moment, fully revealing the heart of God in flesh and blood humanity.

Jesus' birth and life were not accidental, nor was Jesus' growth purely a matter of personal effort or ethical achievement on his part. God's call came uniquely in Jesus' cells and soul and God provided unique possibilities to the little child of Bethlehem. These possibilities elicited Jesus' unique responsiveness as he matured from childhood to adulthood shaping his personality and commitments around God's vision. God's call and Jesus' response were in synch in Jesus' freedom, creativity, and agency.

Without trying to fathom the metaphysics of incarnation or the mysterious intentionality of God, the divine Christ, and the fully human Jesus are one reality embodying in our fleshly and finite world God's vision for history and humankind within the trajectory of the Jewish people. You can't separate the historical Jesus and the cosmic Christ or post-Easter savior. Jesus' uniqueness as God's Christ does not exclude other revelations in other cultures nor does it nullify God's revelation to the Jewish people.

The incarnation claims that Jesus was the spiritual fulfillment of Israel's messianic dream even as God continues then and now to work within Jewish communities.

God is present uniquely in the Healer of Nazareth. A naturalistic Christology, affirming the continuity of God's presence in Jesus with God's presence in our own lives does not preclude special moments of revelation and unique and creative responses to God. When Jesus says "The Father and I are one" he is expressing a holistic spiritual unity in which God's vision and Jesus' response are in synch, energizing both Jesus' spirit and his physical body. Jesus' ability to heal people's spirits and their social and religious situation along with curing their bodies was grounded in a seamless synchronicity of divine-human call and response. As Alfred North Whitehead notes,

> The essence of Christianity is the appeal to the life of Christ as a revelation of the nature of God and his agency in the world... The Mother, the Child, and the bare manger; the lowly man, homeless and self-forgetful, with his message of peace, love, and sympathy; the suffering, the agony, the tender words as life ebbed, the final despair, and the whole with the authority of supreme victory.[6]

God's earthly dream must embrace and fulfill our humanity to transform us and our planet. "And the Word became flesh and lived among us, and we have seen his glory, the glory as of a father's only son, full of grace and truth." (John 1:14) Our flesh and blood, like Jesus's embodiment, is the temple of God's Spirit, the sanctuary of divine presence urging us to live out God's dream of Shalom in our care for our bodies, commitment to the wellbeing of the bodies of others, and the healing of the planet that gives us life.

God loves the world (John 3:16). That love manifests itself in the ubiquitous and intimate divine aim at beauty in the evolutionary process, God's movements toward health in our physical lives,

---

6   Alfred North Whitehead, *Adventures of Ideas* (New York: Free Press, 1967), 167.

and God's call to moral and spiritual stature in our personal and political activities. Jesus companions us, inspiring and enlivening us, in the challenges of daily life and political activism. As the Parents of Christian theology asserted, Jesus lived through every season of life from birth to death, calling us to manifest this same wholeness and love in our lives. Jesus is the Holy Child whose life and mission become the guidepost for our spiritual adventures as God's holy children. As the Christmas carol affirms:

> Jesus is our childhood's pattern, day by day, like us he grew.
> He was little, weak and helpless,
> tears and smiles like us he knew.
> And he feels for all our sadness,
> And he shares in all our gladness.[7]

Jesus' unity with God is made complete in his identity with humankind and all creation. Christmas like Easter is always contemporary, always challenging, and always addressing us in the faces of those around us. As Mother, now Saint, Teresa of Calcutta notes, God is disguised in the vulnerable and weak. Christ is hidden in the face of the homeless and food insecure as well as the emotional insecurity and need for the adulation of national leaders. The incarnation creates a temple in every home and each body, inviting reverence for this good earth and all God's children. The Word and Wisdom made flesh is the gift that keeps on giving, the gift of Christmas, bringing light and love, to the darkest and most chaotic times.

---

7   Cecil F. Alexander, "Once in Royal David's City."

CHAPTER FOUR

EPIPHANY: CHRIST UNLEASHED

Epiphany is the season of divine manifestation. We wake up and see the world with new eyes. As William Blake notes, when the doors of perception are cleansed, we see the infinity of all creation. Each moment is illuminated. Each encounter a theophany. Each place a window into divinity. Every person a mask of God.

In moments of epiphany, the ordinary becomes mystical. Julian of Norwich, who spent her whole life in a time of pandemic, holds a hazelnut in her hand and discovers that the simple, unnoticed hazelnut is a gift from God, filled with divine energy, and sustained each moment by divine love. Annie Dillard wakes up one morning and experiences the tree with lights:

> Then one day I was walking along Tinker creek and thinking of nothing at all and I saw the tree with the lights in it. I saw the backyard cedar where the mourning doves roost charged and transfigured, each cell buzzing with flame. I stood on the grass with the lights in it, grass that was wholly fire, utterly focused, and utterly dreamed. It was less like seeing than like being for the first time seen, knocked breathless by a powerful glance. The flood of fire abated, but I'm still spending the power. Gradually the lights went out in the cedar, the colors died, the cells un-flamed and disappeared. I was still ringing. I had been my whole life a bell and never knew it until at that moment I was lifted and struck. I have since only very rarely seen the tree with the lights in it. The vision comes and goes, mostly goes, but I live for it, for the moment the mountains open and a new light roars in spate through the crack, and the mountains slam."[8]

---

8   Annie Dillard, *A Pilgrim at Tinker Creek:* New York: Harper Perennial, 2007), 16-36.

Long before Julian and Dillard, Jesus saw glorious growth from a humble mustard seed, five thousand meals from a boxed lunch, and world changers from ambivalent followers. Reality is more than meets the eye, every encounter is a gateway to divinity, and every person the light of God's world.

January 6 ushers in the Feast of Epiphany and for the next several weeks we delight in a cornucopia of divine revelation. The moving images of eternity beckon us moment by moment to embrace the Holy Here and Now. Epiphany is the season of magi, graceful baptism, and earthly transfiguration. Magi from the East, not unlike today's Gandalf, Dumbledore, and Professor McGonagall, appear unexpectedly at Jesus' home, greeting the young child with gifts of gold, frankincense, and myrrh. A star illumines their path, guiding them from their temples and seminaries to a foreign land to give homage to a humble child.

Epiphany is the season of the unleashed, unfettered revelation of Christ. Not bound by doctrine, ritual, institution, or even his own earthly incarnation, Jesus will be found everywhere, illuminating every nook and cranny of the universe for those who have eyes to see and ears to hear. Nothing is unclean nor is anyone tarnished, outside the circles of salvation.

The magi come from afar, strange visitors from another religious tradition, these Zoroastrian sages attuned to the divine light and combatants in the battle of light against darkness, arrive in Jerusalem and turn the religious world upside down.

> In the time of King Herod, after Jesus was born in Bethlehem of Judea, wise men from the East came to Jerusalem, asking, "Where is the child who has been born king of the Jews? For we observed his star at its rising, and have come to pay him homage." When King Herod heard this, he was frightened, and all Jerusalem with him; and calling together all the chief priests and scribes of the people, he inquired of them where the Messiah was to be born. They told him, "In Bethlehem of Judea; for so it has been written by the prophet:

'And you, Bethlehem, in the land of Judah,
  are by no means least among the rulers of Judah;
for from you shall come a ruler
  who is to shepherd my people Israel.'"

Then Herod secretly called for the wise men and learned from them the exact time when the star had appeared. Then he sent them to Bethlehem, saying, "Go and search diligently for the child; and when you have found him, bring me word so that I may also go and pay him homage." When they had heard the king, they set out; and there, ahead of them, went the star that they had seen at its rising, until it stopped over the place where the child was. When they saw that the star had stopped, they were overwhelmed with joy. On entering the house, they saw the child with Mary his mother; and they knelt down and paid him homage. Then, opening their treasure chests, they offered him gifts of gold, frankincense, and myrrh. (Matthew 2:1-11)

We live in a gifted universe, in which God's gifts are globally broadcast, flowing to us and then through us to others. Wisdom teachers from another spiritual tradition possess insights that astound the "chosen" recipients. Revelation detours around Jerusalem to Persia. Perhaps the star was visible over Jerusalem as well as today's Iran. But, certain of their superior pipeline to divine truth, the Jerusalem religious community missed the light that guided foreign feet. They missed the gifts of God right in front of them freely given and kept their meager spiritual own gifts to themselves. At every juncture in Jesus' life, Jesus was a light bearer, revealing the path forward, reminding us of our personal holiness, and exposing our waywardness. Tragically, Jesus' ministry of light was met with violence from those whose power and prestige depended on keeping others in the dark about their divine destiny. Violence and persecution are often the fate of those who challenge the potentates and powers and principalities today. We need only remember Dietrich Bonhoeffer, Oscar Romero, and Martin Luther

King not to mention Rosa Parks, John Lewis, and Daniel Berrigan and today's Black Lives Matter protesters.

THE EPIPHANY HOPE

Forty days after his birth, Jesus' parents present him at the Temple. (Luke 2:22-38) Their sacrifice is meager, befitting the salt of the earth, two young pigeons, in contrast to the lamb sacrificed by persons of financial resources. The family is unnoticed in the Temple precincts, just another working-class family bringing their child to be blessed. Only two elders who had lived decades in hope of the Messiah look beyond their poverty to see the holiness of the child and his parents. Epiphanies come unexpectedly and without prior spiritual qualification. The doors of perception are suddenly thrown wide open. Epiphanies also occur as a result of our cleansing the doors of perception so that we can see God when he appears – as God always does – making ordinary flesh and blood the holy of holies. For decades, Anna and Simeon had practiced the presence of God, and their commitment to live more deeply and see more fully opened their senses to God's appearance in an ordinary family.

> Now there was a man in Jerusalem whose name was Simeon; this man was righteous and devout, looking forward to the consolation of Israel, and the Holy Spirit rested on him. It had been revealed to him by the Holy Spirit that he would not see death before he had seen the Lord's Messiah. Guided by the Spirit, Simeon came into the temple; and when the parents brought in the child Jesus, to do for him what was customary under the law, Simeon took him in his arms and praised God, saying,
>
>> "Master, now you are dismissing your servant in peace,
>>   according to your word;
>> for my eyes have seen your salvation,
>>   which you have prepared in the presence of all peoples,
>> a light for revelation to the Gentiles
>>   and for glory to your people Israel." (Luke 2:25-32)

God's revelation comes in its fullness to women as well as men. Gender, age, and sexuality are equally blessed by God's presence. In the spirit of Israel's prophets, Anna speaks for God, revealing what others could – or would – not see.

> There was also a prophet, Anna the daughter of Phanuel, of the tribe of Asher. She was of a great age, having lived with her husband seven years after her marriage, then as a widow to the age of eighty-four. She never left the temple but worshiped there with fasting and prayer night and day. At that moment she came, and began to praise God and to speak about the child to all who were looking for the redemption of Jerusalem. (Luke 2:36-38)

Anna and Simeon remind me of a woman described by Sojourners founder Jim Wallis. Each day she greets everyone who comes down the food line at the soup kitchen with a smile and a kind word. When asked why she greets these forgotten and often unkempt people so joyfully, she responded with the affirmation that "one day Jesus is coming down the line and I want to treat him real good."

The practice of Epiphany is eyes open and heart open. It is training to see deeply and differently. Epiphanic vision involves recognizing with Jacob at Beth-El that every place is a gateway to heaven and a house of God. Epiphanic spirituality transforms our vision from "God is in this place – and I did not know it" to "God is here and I'm ready to respond."

GROWING IN WISDOM AND STATURE

All life is call and response. God's vision addresses us each moment of the day and in every moment of experience. Jesus was always a work in process. Jesus' experience and spiritual growth were never complete. The glory of God is fully alive human, fully open to the range of emotions, evolving intellectually, expanding in compassion, and deepening spirituality. Jesus' unity with God is found in his openness to creative transformation and willingness to be aligned with God's will in moments of joy and challenge. When Luke says Jesus "grew in wisdom and stature and favor with God and humankind," he is witnessing to Christ in process, an evolving and growing sense of God's call and a growing congruence with God's vision. (Luke 2:52) Just as God has new experiences and can be novel in God's responses to the world, Jesus grew, expanded his experiences of the world, and responded in creative and compassionate ways to his encounters with friend and foe alike.

In the Temple, the twelve-year-old Jesus listened to the spiritual leaders of his faith tradition. He wanted to grow spiritually and intellectually, and so in question and answer sessions with rabbinical sages, his sense of calling was refined and oriented.

As the One who calls to do greater things, Jesus calls us to embody stature and wholeness similar to his own. We embody the Spirit of Jesus when we make a commitment to personal growth and global responsibility. Like Jesus, we need to plumb the depths of faith and be willing to grow in relationship with contrasting voices. According to frontier process theologian Bernard Loomer:

> By size I mean the stature of a person's soul, the range and depth of his love, his capacity for relationships. I mean the volume of life you can take into your being and still maintain your integrity and individuality, the intensity and variety of outlook you can entertain in the unity of your being without feeling defensive or insecure. I mean the strength of your spirit to encourage others to become freer in the development of their diversity and uniqueness.[9]

Jesus grew intellectually, spiritually, relationally, and ethically, and as the image of human wholeness, God invites us to a life of growth and empathy. Childhood nurture, baptism, repentance, and commitment are the beginning of our journey and Jesus' journey as well. Apart from the birth stories and the account of the twelve-year-old Jesus in Jerusalem, Jesus' growth from childhood to

---

9 Harry James Cargas and Bernard Lee, (*Religious Experience and Process Theology*. Mahweh, NJ: Paulist Press. 1976), 70.

adulthood is a mystery. Jesus truly does come to us one unknown on the seashore of our spiritual lives.

The last hundred years have led to speculation that Jesus may have studied in India, Iran, and Egypt, that he was part of the Essene community, and that he synthesized the wisdom of yogis, Brahmin, monks, rishis, and sages with the prophetic spirit of Judaism. Perhaps, as one Zoom seminar member averred, he never left home as a young man and simply learned his father's trade and discovered his vocation in making furniture and doing business with his neighbors. There is no definitive account of these "lost years" of Jesus. The best we can say is that Jesus grew in wisdom and stature and favor, that is, alignment with God's vision such that he could affirm his spiritual unity with his Parent. We can imagine Jesus growing in moral and prophetic imagination, empathy, compassion, and ability to use the energies of life to cure bodies as well as spirits. We can visualize Jesus interacting with sages and priests as he did in Jerusalem, asking and sharing, and growing through dialogue. We can visualize Jesus seeing his own creativity as a carpenter as a reflection of God's saving creativity in bringing order out of chaos and beauty out of randomness. We can imagine Jesus' circle of compassion expanding to embrace all sentient beings, going beyond nationalism and anthropocentrism.

From the perspective of process theology, Jesus' growth mirrors God's dynamic and evolving experience of the universe. While the circle of God's compassion and providence are universal and ubiquitous, embracing every creature, God's experience and action in the world are constantly changing, A living God is constantly adjusting and readjusting God's vision of possibility to respond to the decisions of human and non-human creatures as well as human institutions. God is infinitely empathetic and flexible to bring forth the best possibilities for any given creature or community. The best possibilities in certain situations may not always be ideal. But, as the ultimate relativist, intimately involved in every moment of our lives, God never gives up on any of us. No perfect and unambiguous possibility may be available to a political leader guilty of fomenting racism and our racial and cultural division. Yet, God still seeks this leader's conversion and over time may effect changes in their life and policies. An abusive spouse may not change overnight, but in the matrix of relationships, God is luring both the abusive spouse and the one who abused toward healthy agency, which may include the dissolution of the marriage. Working for wholeness in all things, God may be calling one to leave the relationship and the other to recognize their emotional disease and seek professional help.

The account of Jesus' response to the Syrophoenician woman, whose daughter suffered from seizures identified at the time with demonic possession, and Jesus' prayer for deliverance from the Cross suggest that Jesus, at times, struggled to fully align himself with God's vision. (Mark 7:24-30) By her pleas, the loving non-Jewish mother may have invited Jesus to expand his level of concern for non-Jews. In the Garden, Jesus struggled with survival just as we do, but made the commitment to transcend self-interest to promote global healing. (Luke 22:22-24) A living Christ embodies all-embracing empathy and concern, appropriate to his social, political, and personal context. Never abstract, Jesus' response to the hopes and fears of humankind was personal, concrete, and invitational. Never coercive, Jesus came as one of us, seeking to elicit healing and wholeness for all humanity personally and communally.

In our Zoom seminar at South Congregational Church, one of the participants asked, "Why did Mary and Joseph get so anxious when they were separated from Jesus? Why did they criticize him when they found him at the Temple? Did they forget the angelic visits, dreams, and magi?" (Luke 2:41-52) Now, while we can't fully experience their anxiety or concern, perhaps Mary and Joseph's response reflect the vacillating nature of mystical experience as well as their concern for their son's wellbeing. We experience the holy – see the divine in a hazelnut and the light of the world shining through a tree in our garden – and then our life-changing moments of transcendence fall into the background, eclipsed by the daily chores of work, relationships, and family life. We are forever changed. Yet the glory of God can never constantly be sustained in finite and distracted human experience. The Temple incident concludes with Mary once again remembering the uniqueness of her child as she treasures this and other childhood experiences in her heart. We are always on holy ground, and sometimes we notice it. Jesus' growth, even on the verge of adulthood, reminds us that insight and inspiration are always a moment away, that questioning and listening are essential to becoming Christlike, and that spiritual growth, while fed by transcendent moments, is a day-to-day affair of cultivating the sacrament of the present moment (Jean-Pierre de Caussade), knowing our spiritual insights come and go, but deep down forever change us.

BELOVED AND BAPTIZED

Mirroring the biblical witness, process theology affirms the relational nature of life. The whole universe conspires to create each moment of experience and each moment of experience radiates across the universe. The Baptism of Jesus reveals his unique relationship with God, but his uniqueness is also ubiquitous. Jesus is not an anomaly, unrelated to our daily lives, but our childhood's pattern and the lure of spiritually and relationally mature adulthood.

It is appropriate that Jesus chooses to mark this rite of vocational and spiritual passage with his prenatal companion John the Baptist. We don't know the nature of their relationship. But, I imagine them staying in touch through the years, recognizing their unique relationship with God and each other, and sharing each other's spiritual adventures. Did they study together in the Essene monasteries? Did they share each other's spiritual visions? Did John see himself as Jesus' way maker preparing the spiritual path for his ministry? In John, we see a prophetic spirit, separating the wheat from the chaff and pronouncing judgment on the nation. We also see someone with great hope that people can repent, change their lives, and align themselves with God's vision. In John, we also see one who is willing to let go of his own ego, whose humility allows Jesus to take center stage as God's embodiment of the age of Shalom.

At his baptism, Jesus receives further confirmation of his relationship with God. More than that, his encounter with the Holy One expands his growing sense of vocation as God's messenger and savior. Jesus does not need to be baptized, nor is baptism a necessity for God's love, our hospitality, or obtaining otherworldly salvation. Jesus' baptism and ours can be theophanies in which we encounter the Loving God and receive our calling to be God's companions, each in our unique way, in healing the world. For those baptized as infants, baptism reminds us throughout our lives that we are chosen by God and that God's love is not dependent on any achievement on our part. We are loved and inspired by God regardless of who we are or what we do in the course of our lifetimes. Epiphanic in nature baptism wakes us up to God's all-encompassing love, always ready to embrace, heal, and transform.

The simplicity of Mark's description of Jesus' baptism joins the personal, relational, and political:

> In those days Jesus came from Nazareth of Galilee and was baptized by John in the Jordan. And just as he was coming up out of the water, he saw the heavens torn apart and the Spirit descending like a dove on him. And a voice came from heaven, "You are my Son, the Beloved; with you I am well pleased."

Once again, we are confronted with the stark political realities of history. "In those days," the days of John the Baptist's mission, the days of Roman occupation and Herodian oppression, Jesus is baptized. Jesus' baptism and ours are always historical, contextual, and personal, emerging in our place and time and calling us forward toward new horizons of spiritual commitment. Baptism reveals and transforms. When Jesus rose from the water, he received a divine revelation. The world is transfigured, and God speaks through cloud and dove. Perhaps now more than ever Jesus experienced himself as God's Child, Beloved by the Parent, and being prepared by the Divine Parent to live out his vocation. This is not a new reality, created by the ritual of baptism, but Jesus' ultimate identity. Still, the Spirit's descent and the Divine Word's revelation awaken Jesus to new possibilities. The implicit becomes explicit. God's graceful initiatives, the call and response that has been at work over the past three decades, come to fullness, and with them the call to mission.

Jesus' baptism is a rite of passage, an opening to deeper spiritual energies. It is not an antidote for the human condition or original sin, or a necessity for salvation for us or Jesus. Jesus' baptism is a sacramental act in a sacramental universe, a holy act in an already holy universe. A saving act in a world where God wants to save all. We are God's children, revealing God's original wholeness in our depths, the counterforce to the brokenness of life.

The call and response of baptism is revealed in both infant and adult or believers' baptism. On the one hand, God's call comes apart from any effort or achievement on our part. The Loving Parent, like every loving parent, embraces their child out of pure grace and love. God pronounces "you are my beloved on every child." Jesus knew himself to be loved infinitely and unconditionally and shared that infinite and intimate love with humankind. Later, whether through confirmation, believer's baptism, or personal renewal, we claim the grace that guides us from our birth and accept the love that empowers us to become lovers of the world. Jesus loved infinitely, and his love was so great that he challenged his followers to fully embody the light God had given, calling them to discipleship and mission, to be harbingers of God's coming Shalom.

TRANSFIGURING SPIRITUALITY

The Revised Common Lectionary, used by most North American and European Protestant churches, places the Transfiguration of Jesus as the culmination of the Season of Epiphany.[10] What begins with a star concludes with the illumination of Jesus.

> Six days later, Jesus took with him Peter and James and John, and led them up a high mountain apart, by themselves.

10   Other Christians celebrate the Transfiguration during Pentecost.

And he was transfigured before them, and his clothes became
dazzling white, such as no one on earth could bleach them. And
there appeared to them Elijah with Moses, who were talking
with Jesus… Then a cloud overshadowed them, and from the
cloud there came a voice, "This is my Son, the Beloved; listen
to him!" Suddenly when they looked around, they saw no one
with them any more, but only Jesus. (Mark 9:2-4, 7-8)

In this epiphanic experience, three of Jesus' followers discover,
with Gerard Manley Hopkins that "the world is charged with the
grandeur of God" In the interplay of Infinite and Intimate, the
world "flame[s] out, like shining from shook foil." With their
senses opened, Jesus' followers experience Jesus' divine identity in
that moment, arising from his embodiment of God's prophetic
vision of Shalom. More than that, in the context of our own cosmo-
logical understanding, they experience the energy of the big bang,
the inner moral and spiritual arc of evolutionary history, and the
bursting forth of divine creativity in every cell.

Transfiguration transports us to vocation. High on the mountaintop, Jesus can see the contours of Calvary and, descending from
the Mount, he faces the powers of death manifest in the despair of
a parent seeking healing for his epileptic child.

Epiphany transfigures everything for those whose doors of perception have been cleansed. Beyond the ambiguity of history, the
tragedy of pandemic and political violence, and our own tendencies
toward self-interest and self-serving patriotism is the deeper reality
of God's moral and spiritual movement in history, the radiant star
stuff of the big bang, and the cosmic, planetary, and personal movement toward greater and greater complexity and beauty. The season
of Epiphany reminds us that we can experience God in sacraments
and in laboratories and protests. Epiphany transfigures our world,
reveals Jesus' deepest nature as God's loving energy made flesh, and
opens our senses to God-sightings in daily life.

CHAPTER FIVE

LENT: FULL HUMANITY

J esus was fully human. His unique relationship with God embraced the totality of human experience from conception to death. The word was made flesh, with all the joys and complications of embodiment. The Word incarnate in Jesus was historical, located in space and time, sharing in our common human DNA, social context, and political environment. Jesus ate and drank as we do, and experienced, we suspect, growing pains as a child, weariness after a hard day's work, and the physiological as well as emotional changes of adolescence and adulthood. Although Jesus never married, he may have appreciated the physical and emotional beauty of those around him and pondered the joys of marriage and family.

Jesus as the embodiment of "God in all things" shares the joyful ambiguity of human existence, including the realities of ambivalence, conflict, and temptation faced by all humankind. No doubt alluding to Jesus' incarnation and death as well as his spiritual retreat in the wilderness, the author of Hebrews proclaims:

> he had to become like his brothers and sisters in every respect, so that he might be a merciful and faithful high priest in the service of God, to make a sacrifice of atonement for the sins of the people. Because he himself was tested by what he suffered, he is able to help those who are being tested. (Hebrews 2:17-18)

Jesus' embrace of the fullness of human experience extends to his spiritual and emotional life:

> For we do not have a high priest who is unable to sympathize with our weaknesses, but we have one who in every respect has been tested as we are, yet without sin. (Hebrews 4:15)

Jesus' everyday life and lifelong experience testify to the affirmation "God in all things, all things in God." Early Christian theologians asserted that Jesus' complete identification with human joy and suffering throughout all the seasons of life made every season of our lives holy and transparent to divinity. Lent, like Christmas, is a season of full immersion in human existence, inviting us to be fully human, that is, to explore the wonder and complexity of our lives and relationships, as we embrace God's presence in our cells as well as our souls. Jesus was tempted and tested and yet saw his embracing his challenges and conflicts as a pathway to full identification with both God and humankind.

ASHES OF PROMISE

Each Ash Wednesday, Christians across the globe gather to acknowledge our mortality and imperfection. We recognize the ambiguity of life and the reality that even our best intentions can create pain for ourselves and others. Looking into the mirror of mortality, we are aware of the brevity of our years and know that in the midst of life we are surrounded by death, as the Reformer Martin Luther asserts. We recognize our limitations and fallibility. Our hope is that as we confront our mortality with God as our companion, we will discover, with Luther, that in the midst of death, we are also surrounded by life.

My own emphasis as a liturgist and preacher on Ash Wednesday follows the scripture "now is the day of salvation." (2 Corinthians 6:2) As I place ashes on congregants' foreheads, I announce "Repent and believe the good news" as a reminder that in this holy moment we can open to God's grace, let go of the past, and embrace God's "call forward," as John Cobb notes, toward greater compassion and agency in changing our lives and the world.

Lent is the season of holistic and embodied repentance, of turning away from our waywardness, abandoning our self-interest, and letting go of our sense of privilege in favor of recognizing our solidarity with all who suffer, grieve, and bring pain to others. Lent is a call to creative transformation in our personal and political lives. Ash Wednesday and Lent invite us to an examination of conscience, taking a close look in the mirror of our lives noting where we as persons, congregations, and nations have abandoned the divinely-inspired moral arc of history moving through our politics and personal life in favor of self-interest that leaves in its wake an endangered planet, social, racial, and economic injustice, and the stunting of millions of youthful spirits.

We are destined for greatness. We are a little less than divine and yet we squander our divinity in foolish schemes, alienation, and denigration of our neighbor, irresponsible consumerism, institutional violence, and reckless incivility. Though endowed with the divine spirit and bearing the image of God as our deepest reality, physical death is an eventuality for all of us and sadly we perpetrate death on those around us by our attitudes and behaviors. Tragically, we often choose the pathways of death in our personal, relational, and corporate lives, when abundant life is constantly being offered to us. Even if we have a heavenly destiny, we need to "number our days" to gain a heart of wisdom and rejoice in our unique and precious life.

The ashes with which the Lenten journey begins remind us that like us, Jesus was fully human, a child of dust, tempted and tried, fully embedded in the challenges of mind, body, spirit, and relationships that we face. Lent reminds us of promise, possibility, and peril. We can embrace God's call, doing something beautiful for our Creator and the world, and we can also turn from God's vision of Shalom. We can recognize our solidarity with all creation or use our freedom to victimize others. Our mortality can inspire us to live fully in the moment, remembering "this is the day that God has made, let us rejoice and be glad in it." Our mortality can also tempt us to individualistic and nationalistic self-interest, believing that security and power can ensure the immortality of our individual lives and institutions. A child of dust, Jesus was also the incarnation of star stuff, the energy of love that created and evolved the universe. Living out the divine lure toward full humanity amid the conflicts and wonders of historical experience, Jesus placed the totality of his experience in God's care, aligning his decision-making and response to the world with God's moment-by-moment dream of Shalom.

TEMPTATION AND GRACE

Jesus lived in solidarity with ambiguous humankind. As Philippians 2:5-11 asserts, Jesus' saving power came from his intimate identification with humanity in its greatness and tragedy. Early on, Jesus came to realize that salvation cannot be mediated through cultivating personal or corporate exceptionalism and isolation. Jesus also knew that with greatness – even spiritual greatness – comes great danger and the ability to do great harm. Jesus' spiritual birthright endowed him with unique powers of mind, body, spirit, and relationship.

Greatness requires refining and direction and embracing a realistic sense of possibility and limitation. Every great spiritual leader from Buddha to Mohammed goes through a time of testing in which they are asked, "How will you utilize your great power? Will your power lead to self-aggrandizement or sacrifice for the greater good? Will your power isolate you from others or deepen your empathy with those who struggle daily with temptation, addiction, anger, greed, and political powerlessness? Will you choose the blissful transcendence of heaven and enlightenment over-identification with suffering humankind?"

The baptism of Jesus tore open the heavens, uniting heaven and earth, and revealing Jesus' true nature as God's beloved child. After the ecstasy of theophany, now fully aware of his unique relationship to God and status among his human siblings, Jesus is driven by God's Spirit into the wilderness for a time of retreat, reflection, and refining. The wilderness is the place of threat, where the wild things are. Yet, for great religious teachers as well as political powerhouses, the greatest threats are internal, and involve our choice to orient ourselves toward life or death and self-interest or compassionate healing. If he is to embody God's vision and use God's energy rightly, Jesus' baptismal mysticism and empowerment must be grounded in loyalty to God and the world. He must face the totality of his experience, including the temptations of power, protection, and embodiment, the temptation to avoid life's struggles and dominate others, based on the illusion that transcendent and coercive power can be used in ways that go beyond self-interest.

The Gospel of Mark describes in brief and stark detail Jesus' sojourn into the wilderness:

> And the Spirit immediately drove him out into the wilderness. He was in the wilderness forty days, tempted by Satan; and he was with the wild beasts; and the angels waited on him. (Mark 1:12-13)

"The Spirit immediately drove him into the wilderness." Deep within, Jesus felt the urge for solitary reflection and discernment. Divine wisdom propelled Jesus to a time of self-examination and vocational discovery so that his gifts might be used to heal the world and nurture human freedom, creativity, and agency. Jesus was called to embrace human experience, not dominate it, bringing out the better angels of our nature in accordance with our personal and institutional freedom, and not magisterial compulsion. In the wilderness, Jesus discovered his calling as an artist of the Spirit, evoking within humankind our gifts for the common good and our vocation as Jesus' companions in healing the world.

Matthew and Luke expand on Mark's vision of Jesus' temptations and we must assume that if these temptations have any historical basis, they must have been grounded in Jesus' conversations with his followers. Not exhibitionistic, Jesus nevertheless described his own experiences in ways that would edify his followers, then and now. It is instructive to focus on Matthew's and Luke's unique understandings of Jesus' experience of temptation as pivotal to Jesus' understanding of his mission and ministry as one of us, knowing our experiences from the inside as his own. In the wilderness, Jesus embodied Alfred North Whitehead's description of God as "the fellow sufferer who understands."

> Then Jesus was led up by the Spirit into the wilderness to be tempted by the devil. He fasted forty days and forty nights, and afterwards he was famished. The tempter came and said to him, "If you are the Son of God, command these stones to become loaves of bread." But he answered, "It is written,
>
>> 'One does not live by bread alone,
>> but by every word that comes from the mouth of God.'"
>
> Then the devil took him to the holy city and placed him on the pinnacle of the temple, saying to him, "If you are the Son of God, throw yourself down; for it is written,
>
>> 'He will command his angels concerning you,'
>> and 'On their hands they will bear you up,
>> so that you will not dash your foot against a stone.'"
>
> Jesus said to him, "Again it is written, 'Do not put the Lord your God to the test.'"
> Again, the devil took him to a very high mountain and showed him all the kingdoms of the world and their splendor; and he said to him, "All these I will give you, if you will fall down and worship me." Jesus said to him, "Away with you, Satan! for it is written,
>
>> 'Worship the Lord your God,
>> and serve only him.'"
>
> Then the devil left him, and suddenly angels came and waited on him. (Matthew 4:1-11)

Matthew notes that Jesus' wilderness retreat was shaped by his spiritual practices. Jesus fasted for forty days. Jesus stripped down to the essentials, physically and spiritually, placing himself entirely in divine care, letting go of anything standing between himself and God's vision for his vocation as God's healer and savior. While most progressives lack a theology of a personal devil, a coequal with

God, we certainly know something of the temptations that emerge in our quest for spiritual maturity. We live with our own demons and compulsions that lure us away from God's vision for our individual and relational lives. Our institutions have ideals – think, as an example, of your congregation's mission statement or the USA Declaration of Independence - but succumb to self-interest, privilege, and institutional injustice. Think of the contrast between the USA ideal "all men [persons] are created equal" and its original sins of slavery and the genocide of the First Americans not to mention the continuing injustices women, the LGBTQ community, and persons of color face in our country. Think of political leaders and their followers' inclination to undermine democracy and response to the pandemic for personal political gain.

Process theologian David Griffin describes the demonic as involving undermining God's aim at beauty and wholeness for persons and institutions:

> The demonic involves creaturely power that is exercised in a way that is diametrically opposed to divine purposes… demonic power would involve *creaturely creativity that is exercised on the basis of greed, hate, or indifference, and therefore without the intent to promote the welfare of those affected by it…* that creaturely creativity is *powerful enough to threaten divine purposes.*[11]

The temptation of the demonic involves placing ultimacy in finite things, in unrestrained personal and national self-interest, in the intentional – and often unintentional – destruction of others, both human and non-human for our benefit, and the elevation of nations and politicians to godlike status in the conflation of God and country. The demonic seeks security, prosperity, power, and immortality through the destruction and diminishment of others.

The demonic, as we shall see, is often present in good things, even our religious values, that claim false security, certainty, and ultimacy. Jesus' temptations remind us that the greatest evils are

11   David Ray Griffin, *The Christian Gospel for the Americas: A Systematic Theology* (Anoka, MN: Process Century Press, 2019), 224.

often masked by those who claim to be the arbiters of faith and ethics and who are willing to coerce and kill to protect our orthodox faith and parochial values. As Dostoevsky's tale of the "Grand Inquisitor" suggests, the demonic may be present in the machinations of religious institutions whose allegiance to the status quo is greater than their openness to God's constant process of creative transformation. As a result of its marriage of faith to coercive power, authoritarian religious orthodoxy in the United States and across the globe may be – along with nationalism and racism – the most dangerous manifestation of the demonic in our world. The demonic use of religion is not restricted to Christianity but is found in any religious ideology that places doctrine, power, and abstract ethical norms ahead of concrete, inclusive, dynamic, and forward movement of God's Spirit in the world.

Luke adds a slightly different order and interpretation of Jesus' experiences in the wilderness. Like Matthew, Luke recognizes the reality of demonic temptation to distort our personal ethics and political policies.

> Jesus, full of the Holy Spirit, returned from the Jordan and was led by `the Spirit in the wilderness, where for forty days he was tempted by the devil. He ate nothing at all during those days, and when they were over, he was famished. The devil said to him, "If you are the Son of God, command this stone to become a loaf of bread." Jesus answered him, "It is written, 'One does not live by bread alone.'"
>
> Then the devil led him up and showed him in an instant all the kingdoms of the world. And the devil said to him, "To you I will give their glory and all this authority; for it has been given over to me, and I give it to anyone I please. If you, then, will worship me, it will all be yours." Jesus answered him, "It is written,
>
>> 'Worship the Lord your God,
>>   and serve only him.'"

Then the devil took him to Jerusalem, and placed him on the pinnacle of the temple, saying to him, "If you are the Son of God, throw yourself down from here, for it is written,

'He will command his angels concerning you,
        to protect you,'
And 'On their hands they will bear you up,
        so that you will not dash your foot against a
stone.'"

Jesus answered him, "It is said, 'Do not put the Lord your God to the test.'" When the devil had finished every test, he departed from him until an opportune time. (Luke 4:1-13)

Luke recognizes the ambiguity of all human and perhaps divine enterprises. Jesus' temptations revolve around good things – security, the use of power in the public and religious sphere, and comfort and sustenance. Food, power, and security are all to be valued and are in varying degrees necessary for a good life. Yet, they can get in the way of our vocation as God's beloved companions when they become objects of our ultimate concern. Jesus struggled with them just as we do. Power can corrupt. Revolutions seeking justice can become agents of violence and repression. Safety for our families can lead to institutional violence meted out to persons of color, immigrants, and political opponents. A plentiful diet may involve stressing the environment with fertilizers and over-planting, unjust distribution of food reserves, and disease ironically due to both malnutrition and obesity. We need to live simply so others might simply live.

The fully human Jesus faced the temptation to establish God's realm coercively, supplanting the Romans violently through the binary ideology of us versus them, assuming we are the righteous ones in contrast to the moral bankruptcy of those we oppose. Jesus did not opt for the political status quo. In fact, his open table and inclusive relationality were grounded in the vision of God's realm on earth as it is heaven. Jesus was crucified, in part, because his mission threatened both religious and secular power. Still,

Jesus recognized that God's sun and rain fell on the righteous and unrighteous alike. Redemption is possible for our political as well as personal opponents. All of us stand in the need of grace. Even Jesus requires angelic support to face the temptations of the wilderness.

Power is essential to human relationships. But power often corrupts. Our most altruistic goals, even Christian goals, can be subverted by the quest to have secular power. The way of Jesus is political though not partisan. Following Jesus changes our values, lifestyle, relationships, commitments, and voting patterns. There is a temptation, however, to use power – even for what we assume to be positive ends – coercively. When a politician running for USA President promises a Christian crowd, "Christianity will have power. If I'm there, you will have plenty of power, you don't need anybody else," his words mimic that of Satan's temptations in the wilderness. With coercive power, we can establish a Christian nation. But this power will eventuate in violence, as it always does, toward dissenters and outsiders – persons who hold different religious beliefs, members of the LGBTQ community, critics, and those who have differing moral and political positions. Sadly, it appears that many conservative and so-called "orthodox" Christians have sold out their integrity to have a place at the political table, secure a Supreme Court justice, or defy standards of safety in a time of pandemic.

In contrast, the power of Jesus is kenotic and relational, grounded in an all-inclusive vision of Shalom which inspires us to widen the circle of love and awaken positive power from diverse communities. Grounded in hope in God's Beloved Community, we can be politically active while recognizing diverse opinions and lifestyles and finding ways to inspire wholeness and community in the body politic.

Physical well-being is important. Our desire for security and safety can provoke violence and alienation toward those we deem to be threats. Witness the unprovoked attacks on African Americans, Asian Americans, and members of the LGBTQ+ community during the Coronavirus pandemic. Our quest for absolute security leads us to cling to the status quo, assuming that business as usual in our communities, churches, and nation will protect us from unwanted changes. Still, most hills – success, wealth, adulation - are not worth dying on. If we hold on too closely to our lives, making safety and security the criterion for wellbeing, we will deaden our spirits. Martin Luther King captures the contrasting poles of life – survival and sacrifice – in a speech he gave in Memphis, Tennessee, not knowing consciously that he would be assassinated the next day.

> Well, I don't know what will happen now. We've got some difficult days ahead. But it really doesn't matter with me now, because I've been to the mountaintop. And I don't mind. Like anybody, I would like to live – a long life; longevity has its place. But I'm not concerned about that now. I just want to do God's will. And He's allowed me to go up to the mountain. And I've looked over. And I've seen the Promised Land. I may not get there with you. But I want you to know tonight, that we, as a people, will get to the Promised Land. So I'm happy, tonight. I'm not worried about anything. I'm not fearing any man. Mine eyes have seen the glory of the coming of the Lord.[12]

Perhaps Jesus remembered his temptations in the wilderness as he prayed in the Garden of Gethsemane. Perhaps the Garden was the "opportune time" for demonic temptation, noted by Luke. Like Martin Luther King, Jesus wanted to live. As an agent of his own destiny, he did not have to travel the way of the Cross. He could have imagined a longer life as a noted rabbi and healer with wife and family. Yet, he followed God's vision, sacrificing an array of positive possibilities to align himself with his mission as God's healer and savior in his time and throughout the ages.

> And going a little farther, he threw himself on the ground and prayed that, if it were possible, the hour might pass from

---

12 Martin Luther King, Jr. *Testament of Hope: The Essential Writings and Speeches of Martin Luther King, Jr.* (edited by James M. Washington), (New York: HarperSanFrancisco, 1986), 286.

him. He said, "Abba, Father, for you all things are possible; remove this cup from me; yet, not what I want, but what you want." (Mark 14:35-36)

God's vision inspires and supports freedom and creativity. God's will is providential and not predestining. God's love is all-compassing and constantly at work in the movements of history. God is also, as theologian Thomas Oord asserts, "uncontrolling" in God's love for the world. The shape of Jesus' full humanity and alignment with God was not predetermined but open-spirited and filled with a variety of possible positive paths. In that moment, Jesus saw the impact of his faithfulness on his followers and generations to come. The way of the Cross was not preordained but emerged from Jesus' agency as God's primary manifestation of the way of healing and wholeness.

CLAIMING YOUR VOCATION

After his retreat in the wilderness, the death of John the Baptist calls Jesus to public ministry. He has completed his spiritual apprenticeship and is now ready to move to center stage as God's healer and savior. Jesus faced his temptations and was insofar as is possible transcended his needs for adulation and domination. His loyalty is now to God and the world. Mark succinctly describes the beginning of Jesus' public ministry.

> Now after John was arrested, Jesus came to Galilee, proclaiming the good news of God, and saying, "The time is fulfilled, and the kingdom of God has come near; repent, and believe in the good news." (Mark 1:14-15)

Claiming our vocation is good news. Jesus' embodiment of God's vision brings God's realm near. We can glimpse in Jesus' ministry and mission the horizons of God's realm. Within Jesus' vocational affirmation, we can see the energetic movements of the moral and spiritual arcs of history inspiring healers, justice-seekers, and protesters.

Fresh from his wilderness sojourn and rejuvenated by God's affirmation of his identity as Beloved Son, Jesus preaches his first sermon at his hometown, Nazareth. Jesus' spiritual retreat enabled him to become a channel of the prophetic spirit and incarnation of the divine pathos. Filled with the Spirit, Jesus proclaims the embodiment of Isaiah's vision as a counterforce to the violence of Roman occupation and Temple complicity. He claims one of his vocations, as N.T. Wright suggests, the role of a first-century Hebrew prophet.

> "The Spirit of the Lord is upon me,
>   because he has anointed me
>   to bring good news to the poor.
> He has sent me to proclaim release to the captives
>   and recovery of sight to the blind,
>   to let the oppressed go free,
>   to proclaim the year of the Lord's favor." (Luke 4:18-19)

The holistic spirituality of Jesus' first message embraces the personal and political, taking us beyond isolated individual salvation to global healing. Although Jesus' holistic spirituality does not prescribe specific forms of public policy and goes beyond partisan ideologies, the clear ethical and political bias, emerging from Jesus' prophetic spirituality, challenges systemic poverty, injustice, and oppression. God's Jubilee turns upside down every structure of inequality and exclusion, challenging us to a politics of restoration and transformation.

JESUS' LENTEN SPIRITUALITY

Jesus pioneers a contemplative activism. Jesus' energetic social and spiritual activism rises from the springs of solitude. His solitary prayer life finds fulfillment in expanding the circles of compassion, hospitality, and healing. Mark describes Jesus' balance of contemplation and action in his portrayal of a "day in the life" of Jesus. (Mark 1:21-39) After a day of teaching, preaching, healing, and

pastoral visitation, Jesus retreats to a solitary place to recalibrate
his Spiritual GPS.

> In the morning, while it was still very dark, he got up and
> went out to a deserted place, and there he prayed. And Simon
> and his companions hunted for him. When they found him,
> they said to him, "Everyone is searching for you." He answered,
> "Let us go on to the neighboring towns, so that I may proclaim
> the message there also; for that is what I came out to do." And
> he went throughout Galilee, proclaiming the message in their
> synagogues and casting out demons. (Mark 1:35-39)

Jesus was a person of prayer and models a holistic vision of
prayer for those who choose to follow his Way. For Jesus, the journey
inward and outward is part of a dynamic rhythm of contemplation
and action overcoming our binary separation of faith and politics,
sacred and secular, prayer and protest, and heaven and earth. Jesus'
Lenten journey was a pivotal moment in his growing in wisdom
and stature. In the silence of the wilderness, he encountered the
wild beasts within himself, the deep passions of survival, power, and
enjoyment, and integrated them with the even deeper passions for
justice and love characteristic of the Abba whose love chose him
and whose mission Jesus is now choosing. He discovers that there
is only "one world," that this world is a thin place transparent to
the divine, inspiring us to incarnate God's vision "on earth as it is
in heaven."

Jesus' Lenten spiritual disciplines enabled him to grow in wisdom and in stature throughout his lifetime. (Luke 2:52) Jesus'
commitment to holistic and embodied spirituality widened his
soul and opened him to the pain and joy of the world. Like the
Hebraic prophets who embraced the "divine pathos," described by
Abraham Joshua Heschel, Jesus' inner life inspired greater empathy
and engagement with the world. In moments of meditative prayer,
Jesus felt both the peace that passes understanding, the stillness
of the divine center, as well as the restlessness of God's quest for
justice and Shalom. Jesus' confrontation with his temptations and
his commitment to prayerful unity with God's vision enabled him

to make Holy Week the Way of the Cross the Way of Healing and Salvation.

LENTEN ACTIVISM

Contemplation leads us from apathy to empathy and passivity to agency. Prayer eventuates in lament and protest. Jesus' spiritual life opens rather than closes him to the pain and injustice of the world. The Galilean healer weeps over Jerusalem and then turns over the merchandizing tables in the Jerusalem Temple as a sign of God's judgment on religiously grounded injustice and the alliance of religious leaders to Roman oppression.

As we will discover in the next chapter, Holy Week is an everyday reality for a large segment of humankind. Every day millions are traumatized and with each act of violence and injustice committed interpersonally or by political structures, Christ is crucified. Lent leans toward Holy Week, challenging us to face our own personal and national temptations and choose life for our loved ones and the planet. Lenten spirituality is embodied in active commitment to simplicity of life, in spiritual decluttering, which contributes to the wellbeing of the least of these, whether in our individual lives or political involvement not to mention environmental healing. Jesus' wilderness spirituality also inspires him – and us – to challenge the pretense of the wealthy and powerful and to constantly examine our own complicity in injustice. Recognizing our temptations – as Jesus did – helps immunize us – or makes us aware of our temptations - to complacency and normalizing personal and structural injustice, racism, and violence.

As I write these words, the nation is reeling from another shooting of an African American by police officers. Protesters march through Kenosha, Wisconsin, in the wake of a police officer's shooting Jacob Blake seven times in the back. The seasons of Lent and Holy Week remind us that Jesus' message convicts the perpetrators of violence and injustice and calls us to repent our complicity in structural and social injustice. Jesus' Lenten spirituality, issuing in the conflicts of Holy Week, also speaks to the victims of injustice. As the embodiment of God's commonwealth of Shalom, Jesus stands with all who are victimized – with the victims of sex trafficking, domestic violence, child abuse, political persecution, institutional injustice, science denial, and sexual harassment.

Like his spiritual companion and relative, John the Baptist, Jesus directed most of his moral and spiritual condemnation against the wealthy, powerful, and privileged, to those who perpetrate or turn a blind eye to violence and injustice personally and politically. He called the wealthy to confession and the poor to imagination. In Jesus' first sermon, channeling the voice of the prophet Isaiah, he proclaims his baptismal anointing to heal and empower persons living with disabilities and poverty, political prisoners, and those suffering from social injustice due to oppression, neglect, or institutional injustice. (Luke 4:18-19) His neighbors embrace his message until he universalizes God's grace, asserting that divine inspiration touches foe as well as friend, outsider as well as countryman. (Luke 4:24-30) God's Spirit embraces equally persons and communities, black and white, heterosexual and LGBTQ, able-bodied and disabled, but the Spirit's healing touch falls most particularly on those abused, excluded, and violated. They need comfort and support, but more importantly liberation to become agents of their destiny as God's beloved children.

The Spirit's healing for the wealthy, privileged, and apathetic comes initially through the shock type of heavenly surgery, as Howard Thurman avers, that awakens us to the pain of the world and compels us to become healers ourselves if we choose to live in the way of Jesus. The wealthy and powerful have to divest and declutter so others may simply live and then chart a course toward sharing power with the least of these, vulnerable, traumatized, and forgotten. Our response to God's call to repent, and forsake the ways of injustice and planetary destruction, brings new hope to victims of injustice. Jesus' solidarity with every form of suffering invites us to solidarity and to vocational commitment in body, mind, spirit, and political action to God's vision of Shalom.

CHAPTER SIX

HOLY WEEK: HEALING THROUGH SUFFERING

oly Week is the ultimate manifestation of divine incarnation in all its embodied messiness, fulfilling the dream of Christmas and the revelation of Epiphany. Holy Week is a theophany from start to finish. But this theophany does not occur on a mountaintop or in a transformed post-mortem spiritual body nor is it frankly a comfortable and placid theophany. Theophanies, manifestations of the divine, can be tragic as well as ecstatic. The theophany of Holy Week bursts forth in the messiness of conflict and celebration, protest, and politics. The word made flesh suffers in the world of flesh. The one who tents among us feels the agony of rejection and abandonment. The cross on Calvary is the cross at the heart of God, a call to solidarity with all who suffer and a protest on God's behalf against all those who perpetrate the religion and politics of suffering. The cross embodies the spirit of hate whether in Jerusalem, Auschwitz, or today's USA children's detention centers, police killings, or synagogue bombings. You can find Jesus suffering in the concentration camp and on the lynching tree.[13] The cross also embodies the spirit of sacrifice, of God's healing through suffering, Nelson Mandela on Robbin Island, Dorothy Day protesting injustice, John Lewis marching for voting rights, medical workers confronting COVID

---

13 I am indebted to the insights of James Cone, *The Cross and the Lynching Tree* and Howard Thurman, *Jesus and the Disinherited* for their connection of the cross and ministry of Jesus with African Americans as well as their understanding of the cross as a challenge to transformation and solidarity with all who suffer injustice, marginalization, and powerlessness through the machinations of governments, churches, and disease.

19, and family members and spouses caring for a seriously ill or vulnerable child or adult.

Emmanuel, "God with us," is fully incarnate throughout Holy Week. Unless God shares our joys and sorrows, God cannot be one with us. In Holy Week, we discover God's omniscience goes beyond timeless and transcendent observation from a distance. The all-knowing God experiences the world one moment at a time, including the moment-by-moment train wreck of Holy Week. Jesus' tears are real tears. Jesus' pain is real pain. Jesus' death is real death, touching the heart of God. For God is, as Alfred North Whitehead, "the fellow sufferer who understands" and the companion who rejoices.

The babe in swaddling clothes, nursing at Mary's breast, is plunged thirty-three years later into incarnation in its most brutal form. The victim of violence and state-sanctioned murder. Like George Floyd, gasping for breath on Memorial Day 2020, Jesus called out desperately to his Abba. Like Floyd and other victims of state-sponsored violence and ethnic supremacy, Jesus couldn't breathe as crucifixion sucked the life out of him.

Incarnation embraces the totality of life in its tragic beauty and wondrous messiness. Incarnation is painful and messy and yet we can be saved only if God's fleshly Word touches us at our worst and weakest as well as our noblest and strongest. The Word, present in Jesus' Holy Week adventures, is found today in a grandparent dying alone of COVID-19 and the family forbidden to sit at his bedside; the peaceful protester being tear-gassed to facilitate a presidential photo opportunity; the African American man stalked and murdered for being in the wrong neighborhood; a spouse and her children mourning the death of a law officer, and the transgendered youth beaten on his way home from a party. And, again, it is also found in those who face their personal and national crosses as God's partners in healing the world. Crucifixion was real on Good Friday and Good Friday is recapitulated whenever the powerful sacrifice the vulnerable and powerless for political and economic gain. Incarnation is redemptive from cradle to grave and beyond.

Every act of God, from the big bang to today's prophetic prophets, is meant to promote beauty and healing, and in the ambiguities of life, intended to heal the world.

Like the prophets before him, Jesus' breaking down of barriers of healing and hospitality put him at odds with the Jerusalem religious leadership. The Temple leaders of his time were intimately connected with Roman leadership. Their prosperity and vocational security depended on a positive relationship with Rome, most especially local military and political administrators such as Pilate. While they had profound theological differences with Roman polytheism and their apotheosis of Caesar as divine, and considered the Roman pantheon idolatrous and viewed Romans as unclean, in day-to-day practice the Temple and State were united in purpose, maintaining law and order and ensuring their power and prosperity. The first-century Temple priests were similar to religious leaders in our time who abandon ethical standards and the quest for truth to identify their political leader as God's chosen one, superimposing the faces of potentates and demagogues on the image of Jesus.

Prophetic faith always has a critical edge and a creative distance from politics and religion. Though the economic and political powers can be agents of justice and prosperity and, as such, can be redeemed, their healing can only occur in the wake of confession, repentance, and restoration. What they need to do – let go of power – is the one thing they typically choose not to do. Thus, they must silence anyone who threatens the unjust religious and political systems that ensure their prosperity and power.

In the first and twenty-first centuries, clinging to the status quo and confusing faith with power is a form of idolatry. The conflation of church and state, Rome and Jerusalem, Christian nationalism and American exceptionalism, is a virus that puts the quest for spiritual maturity and social justice at risk. The moment religious and political structures become too closely aligned with one another, certain people, most especially those conflated as rioters and protesters, deviants, persons of other faiths, and ethnic outsiders become expendable. These "nuisances and nobodies," to quote John Dominic Crossan, and provocateurs and pariahs, must be eliminated by the powers that be and their henchmen to ensure the smooth order of liturgy, theology, and economics.

That first Holy week is a roller coaster of spirituality and emotion for Jesus and his followers. Ecstatic and hopeful in the wake of the joy of Palm Sunday, they are plunged into conflict with the Jerusalem religious leaders and eventually witness Jesus' abandonment, arrest, and crucifixion.

The Holy Week theophany leads to atonement but not the atonement grounded in the satisfaction of an angry god or a legal quid pro quo. Theophany leads to experiences of graceful unity and forgiveness, often seen as a novel awareness, but in fact a revelation of what was true prior to the Cross, the amazing reality that God loves us fiercely and intimately and is willing to suffer with us and on our behalf. Holy Week reveals God's solidarity with all who suffer.

Jesus doesn't want to experience pain and death. Still, his death is a matter of choice, of embracing his destiny, rather than a preordained necessity. Holy Week reveals Jesus' intention to participate whole-heartedly, body, mind, and spirit, in human suffering. Jesus sacrifices to enact in flesh and blood God's quest for Shalom in history, identifying with our experiences of pain and sinfulness, and inviting us to become companions in God's aim at healing the world.

Holy Week is embodied atonement or unity with God. While there are many theories of atonement, this process of reconciliation and transformation reflects God's love for all creation and God's desire that we experience wholeness. God is not out to punish us. God is out to love us. The Cross reveals God's love. It does not change God's attitude to humanity, appease God's wrath, or satisfy God's righteousness. It provides new possibilities for healing and transformation. Although Jesus' suffering transforms our lives, God does not need the cross to overcome any estrangement on God's part. God never gives up nor does God's love ever cease – God's

mercies are new every morning, whether in the time of the prophets, the writing of Lamentations, first-century Judea, or our time.

The Cross unequivocally reveals God's companionship and
identification with our pain and sorrow. In being with us as one
with us, God presents us with new and creative possibilities and
the energy and inspiration to choose them for our creative transformation and the healing of our communities. As the culmination
of Holy Week, the cross tells us that God experiences and seeks to
heal our pain. God struggles against the powers of injustice and
chaos and invites us to be God's own incarnate hands and feet in
responding to injustice.

Atonement is sacrificial but the sacrifice is all-encompassing, chosen, holistic, and not transactional. God sacrifices for our
wholeness and challenges us to move sacrificially from individual
self-interest and national exceptionalism to world loyalty. God's
sacrifice inspires and energizes, reveals our sin, and provides a path
for our healing. The cross reminds us that Christ died because of sin
as a matter of his willingness to face the institutional and political
evil of his time and not to appease divine justice, pride, or anger.

THE SPIRITUAL AND RELATIONAL ROLLERCOASTER OF HOLY WEEK

In just one week, a universe of human experience unfolds.
From ecstasy and popularity to agony and abandonment. Jesus
is both the primary actor and receptive witness of the events of
Holy Week. Although John's Gospel portrays Jesus as orchestrating
the events of the week, I suspect John's idealized version of Jesus'
intentionality and power – Jesus' control of the drama of Holy
Week – misses the complexity of Jesus' inner life. Jesus is more than
a spectator, observing the events of Holy Week. He is part of the
action, surely an agent and provocateur, but also totally immersed
in the maelstrom of conflict, celebration, and crucifixion. He reacts
and responds as well as creates and guides the week. His power is
in his receptivity as well as his agency.

Jesus comes to Jerusalem, as Martin Luther King came to Memphis, with a vision of what might transpire. But it's unclear if, despite Jesus' recognition of the risk of his Passover visitation, he is fully in control of the events of the week to come. Martin King went to Memphis to support African American sanitation workers. Perhaps, he also recognized that his presence put his life in danger. But the reward of securing justice and equity outweighed the danger. Death was a possibility as it had been throughout King's public career, but the exact moment was unknown to the civil rights crusader. In similar fashion, while Jesus surely knew the immense personal risk of going to Jerusalem, did he fully know what was to unfold by Thursday? Did he know concretely that he would be arrested, beaten, and crucified? As we will see, Jesus' prayer in the Garden of Gethsemane suggests that the possibility of evading death was available to him. Another way of life and a different outcome may have been available to Jesus as late as Holy Thursday night. Longevity – perhaps marriage, family, and a retreat from the public eye to be a small-town teacher and healer – may have been an option. But, like King, Jesus' identification with God's way, emerging out of his mystical experiences of unity with Abba, compelled him to choose the way of the cross rather than the way of comfort.

There is an open-endedness to Holy Week that we need to recognize as an alternative story to narratives of divine predestination and substitutionary atonement. This open-endedness of Holy Week reveals Jesus as fully alive in his quest to glorify God as well as the agency of Jesus' friends and foes. The characters in Holy Week, the priests, Pilate, the disciples, and women followers, are not merely actors reading their lines. They are decision-makers, choosing their roles, in a story that would transform history. Jesus is not a puppet of divine determinism either. He is creating reality as he goes along, injecting new possibilities, choosing novel and redemptive courses of action, and making history himself. Not fully omniscient in terms of what is to come, but deeply aware of the movements of history and human nature and the powers and principalities, the future is open for Jesus as well. Jesus has an array of options in terms of responding to the Passover week conflicts. Perhaps, although God's omniscience alerts God to the many possibilities and likely outcomes emerging out of each moment of experience, the future is also, to some degree, open to God as well. Did Abba hold out some hope for Jesus' being able to institute God's reign on earth as it is in heaven? Was God seeking a change of heart among the religious leaders, Pilate, and the fickle Passover participants? Was God, to some degree, also making it up as God went along, calling, and then responding to human responses?

THE PROMISE OF PALM SUNDAY

Holy Week begins with affirmation and adulation. Jesus is on the move and change is in the air. The Passover crowds shout "Hosanna," and wave branches of praise. Excitement is in the air as crowd members are marching along with Jesus as a foretaste of spiritual and political transformation. Transformation is on the horizon, but not as the crowd expected. "Praise God and God's Messiah," they shout, believing they are on the cusp of unprecedented change that will turn their political, economic, and spiritual worlds upside down. In some of their imaginations, ten thousand angels wait for their marching orders. Their revolutionary dreams required divinely led violent insurrection. Rome will leave in disgrace and God's political realm will be established in perpetuity. Jerusalem will be restored in its splendor and nations will flock to give glory to the God of Abraham, Isaac, Jacob, Moses, and Jesus.

Yet, the incongruity of the situation must have struck some in the adoring crowd. Jesus enters on a humble donkey, or young colt, the symbol of peace and reconciliation, not violence and coercion. The power of the coming Messiah differs from that of Caesar, Pilate, Herod, or the Temple priests. On Palm Sunday, Jesus reveals a different vision of power – the power of love, forgiveness, and inclusion. Jesus' victory comes from immersion in suffering, and transforming pain and injustice, through loving relationships.

Process theologian Bernard Loomer describes two contrasting visions of power – unilateral, dominating power and relational, cooperative power. Unilateral power is binary, coercive, and potentially violent. It comes from above and acts but does not receive. The experiences of creatures, of our fellow humans and the non-human world, have no impact on those who wield unilateral power. Divine and human potentates choose the future without consultation. Challenge or deviation from the unilateral power leads to punishment, excommunication, or ostracism. The wreckage of history gives evidence of the spiritual and political impact of unilateral power – the Crusades and Inquisition, slavery and the decimation of First Nations peoples, the Stalinist and Maoist purges, the terrorism of Taliban and al Qaeda, political assassinations, federal agents on USA streets, and detention camps in China and in the USA borderlands.

In contrast, relational power affirms diversity and pluralism. Relational power looks for the gifts of diversity, elicits partnerships, changes course as times change, and responds to legitimate critiques. Relational power seeks to transform conflict into contrast, to exercise power responsibly for the wellbeing of all including those who perceive themselves as opponents. Relational power seeks to widen the circle of ethical, political, and spiritual consideration. While relational power can exert political and policing influence in times of social upheaval and national threat, first and foremost it seeks peaceful and conciliatory outcomes. It seeks collaboration and not domination. Relational power assumes in the process of call and response, the importance of agency and alternative visions, that the future is open and determined by the energy and creativity of many actors. Profoundly intentional and imaginative, relational power leads by vision and empathy. The relational leader, whether divine or human, calls forth the gifts of a community with an image of horizons of hope and justice and then responds to the community's or nation's creative alternatives. In times of conflict, relational power seeks to inspire the "better angels of our nature" in the quest for common good in concrete and often imperfect situations.

Paul's vision of Christ in Philippians 2:5-11 captures defin-
itively the spirit of relational power, whether utilized by God or
humankind. Paul's listeners would have had two radically different images in mind as they heard his words, ruthless Caesar who
demanded absolute obedience and loving Christ whose victory
comes through healing and forgiveness that empowers our own
loving response.

> In your relationships with one another, have the same
> mindset as Christ Jesus:
>
> Who, being in very nature God,
>   did not consider equality with God something to be used to his
> own advantage;
>   rather, he made himself nothing
>   by taking the very nature of a servant,
>   being made in human likeness.
>   And being found in appearance as a man,
>   he humbled himself
>   by becoming obedient to death—
>   even death on a cross!
>
> Therefore God exalted him to the highest place
>   and gave him the name that is above every name,
> that at the name of Jesus every knee should bow,
>   in heaven and on earth and under the earth,
> and every tongue acknowledge that Jesus Christ is Lord,
>   to the glory of God the Father. (Philippians 2:5-11, NIV)

We bow before Caesar out of fear, knowing any other response
will lead to punishment and exclusion. In contrast, we bow before
Jesus in love, eager to do Christ's bidding as lovers ourselves who
have received the gift of acceptance, affirmation, and empowerment
to do "greater things" in shaping the world.

For Caesar, life is a zero-sum calculus. Your gain is my loss.
Your power diminishes my power. Contrasting viewpoints must be
neutralized or eliminated. Uniformity and adulation are required.
The way of Caesar, and the image of God as Caesar, has given

birth to authoritarian theological and ecclesiastical systems, heresy hunting and excommunication, demands of strict obedience, denunciation of viewpoints and persons who differ from our established spiritually or politically correct viewpoint.

The way of Jesus takes a radically different approach. Our creativity adds to God's creativity, our healthy use of freedom opens new avenues for divine activity, and our imagination inspires innovative responses from our Creator. Whitehead captures this dynamic call and response in terms of our role in shaping God's heavenly vision in the maelstrom of earthly challenges.

> God's purpose is always embodied in particular ideals relevant to the actual state of the world.... Every act leaves the world with a deeper or fainter impress God. He then passes to his next relation to the world with enlarged, or diminished, presentation of ideal values.[14]

The humble Jesus riding on a colt or donkey inspires a holistic, inclusive vision of power in which God and the world are partners. When we do something beautiful for God, we enhance God's experience of the world, we also awaken new possibilities for God to act in the world. We claim our vocation as God's companions in healing the earth. While acts of injustice and ugliness cannot defeat God, they can defer the divinely inspired moral and spiritual arcs of history as well as bringing ugliness to God's experience and to our fellow humans.

On Palm Sunday Jesus models relational companionship, intentional imagination, and empathetic leadership as the source of true power. Taking us beyond binary win-lose, us-them, active-passive models, Jesus invites us to recognize that "we are the ones we've been waiting for", as poet June Jordan asserts. Our responses to God deepen God's joy and bringing and healing to the world, expanding the circles of creativity, freedom, and healthy agency.

---

14   Alfred North Whitehead, *Religion in the Making* (New York: Meridian Books, 1972), 152.

PROPHETIC CHALLENGE

The incarnation is political and nowhere is the politics of incarnation more evident than in Jesus' conflicts with the Temple and political powers. At the heart of the politics of Holy Week is Jesus' cleansing of the Jerusalem Temple.

> Then they came to Jerusalem. And he entered the temple and began to drive out those who were selling and those who were buying in the temple, and he overturned the tables of the money changers and the seats of those who sold doves; and he would not allow anyone to carry anything through the temple. He was teaching and saying, "Is it not written,
>
> > 'My house shall be called a house of prayer
> > for all the nations'?
> > But you have made it a den of robbers."
>
> And when the chief priests and the scribes heard it, they kept looking for a way to kill him; for they were afraid of him, because the whole crowd was spellbound by his teaching. (Mark 11:15-18)

Jesus' overturning of the marketplace tables embodies prophetic protest. Countercultural in nature, Jesus denounces the conflation of religion and economics sponsored by the Temple leadership. That he sees himself as a representative of the prophetic tradition is evident in Jesus' quoting from Isaiah 56:7 and Jeremiah 7:11.[15] God's house is for all people without reservations. Isaiah portrays God welcoming foreigners and outcasts. In contrast, the mercantile spirit of the Temple marketplace excludes persons who can't afford to purchase appropriate sacrifices and creates sacrificial boundaries based on personal largesse as well as social location. Challenging religious practices that divide people, Jesus asserts that God's way transcends our divisions of economics, race, gender, and ethnicity. Everyone is first class, everyone is in the front row, everyone has tickets to the divine banquet. Jesus' open table includes

---

15   For more context, read Jeremiah 5:5-7, 11 and Isaiah 56:6-8.

welcoming and inclusive worship and celebration, unrelated to divisions of class, ethnicity, economics, or health condition. The widow's mite is as important as the landowner's endowment. The tax collector's "Lord have mercy" touches God's heart with the same sentiment as the righteous believer's "I am thankful that I have followed the law and maintained my purity."

Like Amos eight centuries before, Jesus channels the divine pathos, God's empathy with and anger on behalf of the forgotten, excluded, and impoverished.

> I hate, I despise your festivals,
>   and I take no delight in your solemn assemblies.
> Even though you offer me your burnt offerings and grain offerings,
>   I will not accept them;
> and the offerings of well-being of your fatted animals
>   I will not look upon.
> Take away from me the noise of your songs;
>   I will not listen to the melody of your harp.
>
> But let justice roll down like waters,
>   and righteousness like an ever-flowing stream.
> (Amos 5:21-24)

Jesus' prophetic protest is the last straw. His enactment of divine justice and inclusion pushes his sacerdotal opponents over the edge. They fear that Jesus' message of inclusion will reveal their spiritual bankruptcy and also jeopardize their relationship with Rome. They worry that those who have been the objects of their manipulative religion will see through their schemes and lifeless rituals and demand religious practices that change their hearts and transform their lives. Like Jesus and the prophets of old, the people may even go directly to God, detouring around religious intermediaries and their doctrinal and monetary requirements. Surely Jesus knows the risks he is taking. Arrest, banishment, and death are real possibilities. Yet, Jesus' faithfulness to God's vision – his oneness with God's intent for humankind and the world – demands that he go forward despite the likelihood of conflict and condemnation.

DIVINE PATHOS

Holy Thursday and Good Friday are days of suffering love. Jesus' primary concern as he experiences the likelihood of arrest and crucifixion is to leave a legacy of love for his followers and those, like ourselves, who will claim his way of life as central to our spiritual identities. Though death and abandonment are real possibilities, Jesus does not play the victim. He chooses to teach and to love. He enacts his solidarity with humankind through his Passover celebration and sharing of bread and wine. He recognizes that he is part of his people's story. He has been liberated from bondage in Egypt and though he will be arrested soon, his attitude is that of a free person, fully human, yet living out his vocation to the very end. He trusts that this meal of healing and transformation will be remembered long after the crisis that will take his life and scatter his followers.

It is appropriate that Jesus comes to Jerusalem for the Passover feast. Jesus' whole ministry is aimed at liberation and fullness of life. The Spirit descends on Jesus to release captives and liberate the oppressed. Jesus is a free agent, guided by the confluence of his vision and God's, despite what lies ahead. He is free to share in the anxiety of his followers and to remind them that God is always with them, providing a way where there is no way and a model for spiritual transformation.

While the Gospel of John's collections of Holy Thursday sayings may be a compilation rather than a description of Jesus' words on his last night with his followers prior to his crucifixion, it is clear that Jesus' message is intended to remind his disciples that God is with them, divine inspiration through the Holy Spirit is available at all times, greatness and power lies within them, and that nothing can separate them, not even death, from his love. Jesus recognizes their fallibility. Yet sees greatness within their limitations. His own acquaintance with temptation enables him to recognize that their failure of nerve, and even their abandonment and denial, is not the final story. God will continue to inspire and empower them, working through their fears, grief, and regret, just as God continues to inspire us in all our fallibility and fear. Looking beyond the present conflicts, Jesus has a prayer for all who follow him in the future – for us in the maelstrom of our own lives – that we be inspired by God's Spirit and experience unity of purpose despite our differences.

Jesus breaks bread and drinks wine with his followers as a sign of solidarity. The oneness he experiences with God is ours as well. On the precipice of catastrophe, God is with us providing for our deepest needs.

I must admit that as I penned this book in the heart of the Coronavirus pandemic, I needed eucharistic companionship. Though healthy and active, I had a few risk factors over and above my nearly three score and ten in years. I worried about death and diminishment, about not fulfilling my vocation as pastor, husband, parent and grandparent, teacher, and writer. I needed a daily serving of sanctified bread, embodied grace and healing, for the journey from a Power and Wisdom greater than myself. I needed to know, as Jesus' disciples discovered, that Christ is with me always.

When Jesus says "just as I have loved you, you should love one another," he is proclaiming his "rule of life" and inviting us to remember that love casts out fear. God's love, embodied in his body and blood, his life in its entirety, is our hope in times of conflict and contagion. Love never ends and Jesus' love encompassed his followers in the heights and depths, courage and doubt, that were to come. None of these could nullify Jesus' love for them.

On that Holy Thursday, Jesus prayed. First, he prayed for the unity of his followers then and now. He's praying for us in our profoundly messy, uncivil, divisive, yet beautiful world. He prayed that we experience the same oneness with one another and God that he had. Second, he went to the Garden of Gethsemane to immerse himself in prayer, knowing that arrest, humiliation, and death were likely on the horizon. Like us, he prayed for deliverance from pain, suffering, and death. With tears and anguish, Jesus prays, "Father, if you are willing, remove this cup from me; yet, not my will but yours be done." (Luke 22:42)

The "will of God" is often misunderstood. Many theologians, pastors, and simple believers see the will of God as God's determination of historical events. God's providential will determines best, whether it is life or death or success or failure. They assert that God is in "control" and everything flows from God's hands. In contrast, I believe the will of God, reflected in Jesus' prayer at Gethsemane as well as the Lord's Prayer, "Your kingdom come, your will be done, on earth as it is in heaven." (Matthew 6:10) is moral, spiritual, and inspirational in nature. While God is present as the providential guide of every moment of experience, God does not determine Jesus' or our responses but calls us to faithfulness and love. God seeks our embodiment, through our agency, of God's loving and healing will on earth. God wants us to approximate God's heavenly vision but the contours of embodying God's vision are in our hands. We are, as Teresa of Avila avers, the hands and feet of God.

In the Garden, Jesus has choices. He might imagine, as Nikos Kazantzakis envisages in the *Last Temptation of Christ,* an alternative future to death on the cross – a quiet life of marriage and children, a rabbi, delighting in domestic life with Mary of Magdala. Jesus' freedom to choose existed to the very end. Yet, fully alive to God's vision for him – his destiny as God's beloved – he embraced his vocation regardless of the consequences.

On the eve of his assassination in Memphis, Tennessee, Martin Luther King experienced the same tension between longevity and vocation. It is appropriate that I repeat King's powerful words of sacrificial love, well aware of the consequences of following one's vocation regardless of the consequences.

> Well, I don't know what will happen now. We've got some difficult days ahead. But it doesn't matter with me now. I've been to the mountaintop. And I don't mind. Like anybody, I would like to live a long life. Longevity has its place. But I'm not concerned about that now. I just want to do God's will...

I'm not fearing any man. Mine eyes have seen the glory of the coming of the Lord.[16]

This quote bears repeating because it represents courage despite threat and reflects Jesus' path to Calvary. With eyes on God's horizon of love, Jesus found the inner strength to face what lay ahead for him. Grounded in his alignment with God's vision for his life, he chose love for his followers, persecutors, and us. Jesus' willingness to die on our behalf reflected God's love for him and us, not the anger of a distant parent, and his choice to let go of self-interest to be God's messenger and companion in healing the earth.

HEALING THROUGH SUFFERING

On Good Friday, it is our custom to sing "Were You There When They Crucified My Lord?" While factually speaking, the obvious answer is "no," as Jesus' crucifixion is an event limited in space and time. And yet, the hymn reveals a deep truth, Jesus' ministry, death, and resurrection shape our lives as contemporary vehicles of God's saving love. The cross on Calvary is a "thin place" embracing history in its entirety, where God's love meets the world's suffering.

From the perspective of process-relational theology, the incarnation and crucifixion are naturalistic in character and embodiment. They reveal the nature of God's presence always and everywhere. In contrast to images of supernatural intervention, divine revelations from beyond space and time, violating the intricate interdependence of cause of effect, the cross reveals God's immersion in the messy maelstrom of history. Although some moments such as Jesus' conception and crucifixion uniquely and powerfully reveal God's aim at wholeness and redemption, God's quest for healing, wholeness, redemption, and creative transformation is universal. As Whitehead asserts, the world lives by the incarnation of God. Although the ongoing processes of nature reflect God's redemptive

---

16   Martin Luther King, Jr. *Testament of Hope: The Essential Writings and Speeches of Martin Luther King, Jr.* (edited by James M. Washington), (New York: HarperSanFrancisco, 1986), 286.

providence, the cross uniquely reveals God's suffering-responsive love, the love that brought forth the universe and guides the historical process. God's moral and spiritual arc intensely present in Jesus' birth and ministry are also revealed in Jesus' sacrificial love on the cross. Incarnation is messy in its immersion in the scrum of power politics, violence, and self-interest.

On Calvary's hill, Jesus experienced profound physical and emotional trauma. Tortured and abandoned, Jesus cried out "My God, my God, why have you forsaken me." (Matthew 27:46) Demonic darkness threatened to engulf God's loving light. Invoking the words of Psalm 22:1, Jesus experienced the reality of God's absence. Feeling alone and forsaken, by God and his closest male followers, Jesus' anguish is recapitulated throughout the ages. In every cry of absence, God's voice is heard.

As I prepared for my seminar on "Jesus in the Twenty-first Century," from which this text emerged, I heard the echoes of George Floyd's March 25, 2020 cries of "Mama" and then "I can't breathe." I was overwhelmed with the similarity of Floyd's and Jesus' cries of agony and abandonment. I felt the grief of a congregant whose wife died suddenly a few days after their sixty-eighth anniversary. I empathized with the family unable to visit a dying parent during this time of pandemic. I experienced God's tears in a toddler separated from her parents at a USA immigrant detention camp. I have lifted up moments like these throughout the book because these deaths reflect our daily grief – and God's sorrow – at experiences of crucifixion touching everyday people like ourselves, crucifixions that ripple beyond those who suffer to the heart of God and the national psyche. There was, as William Temple avers, a cross in the heart of God before there was a cross on Calvary's hill.

Atonement, unity with God, comes through God's solidarity with all who suffer, not in God's or our avoidance of suffering. God calls through Jesus' sacrificial love, eliciting responses of repentance and healing. God is truly crucified on Calvary and in every place of hopelessness and despair, creating a way where through the dark valley of death and destruction.

The cross reveals the fullness of Jesus' love for humankind in all its ambiguity and sin. Willing to embrace his destiny as God's beloved child and healer, Jesus faces the agony of Calvary. He did not want to die, nor did he wish to suffer excruciating pain. Still, Jesus placed his suffering and abandonment in God's care. Every aspect of life, even dying and death, can inspire prayerfulness.

To those responsible for his death, Jesus announced, "Father, forgive them, they know not what they are doing." (Luke 23:34) Atonement is offered to all, even those who turn away from God through ignorance or intentionality. Not predestined by God, Jesus' cross offers the possibility of redemption in every season of life, including the dying process and the moment of death. Jesus' death demonstrates the reality that God's solidarity with humankind transcends sin, pain, and death. Truly, as Bonhoeffer affirms, only a suffering God can save. In experiencing God's solidarity in Jesus' suffering, we can face death with courage and hope, affirming that Jesus knows our pain and struggle. As the spiritual says,

> Nobody knows the trouble I see
> Nobody knows but Jesus.

WAITING TO EXHALE

At first glance on Holy Saturday, nothing happens. Jesus is buried in Joseph of Arimathea's tomb. The grave is sealed. Hope has died for Jesus' followers. Their future is as tightly sealed as Jesus' tomb.

We have no idea what – if anything – Jesus experienced in the interim between Good Friday and Easter morning. The only account of Jesus' post-mortem experience is found in I Peter:

> For Christ also suffered for sins once for all, the righteous for the unrighteous, in order to bring you to God. He was put to death in the flesh, but made alive in the spirit, in which also he went and made a proclamation to the spirits in prison, who in former times did not obey, when God waited patiently in the days of Noah, during the building of the ark, in which a

few, that is, eight persons, were saved through water. (I Peter 3:18-20)

The Apostles Creed states that Jesus "descended to the dead" or "descended into hell" to bring good news to those who died prior to his mission to humankind. These passages suggest that Jesus was a conscious agent during this interim period. He was continuing preaching and teaching, bringing God's redemption to persons living in the shadows of Sheol. We would like to know what Jesus experienced in the days following the crucifixion. Was it a time of healing and transformation? Was he disengaged from his body? Did he feel the wounds that were a sign of his identity following the resurrection?

Yet, among those who are part of the solidarity of suffering, there is a deep promise we can trust, as perhaps Jesus did, that God is with us and in life and death, and nothing can separate us from God's loving companionship.

> Where can I go from your spirit?
>   Or where can I flee from your presence?
> If I ascend to heaven, you are there;
>   if I make my bed in Sheol, you are there.
> If I take the wings of the morning
>   and settle at the farthest limits of the sea,
> even there your hand shall lead me,
>   and your right hand shall hold me fast.
> If I say, "Surely the darkness shall cover me,
>   and the light around me become night,"
> even the darkness is not dark to you;
>   the night is as bright as the day,
>   for darkness is as light to you. (Psalm 139:8-11)

In the dark wood in which we like Dante can discern no clear way forward, there is a glimmer of light. Life leans toward resurrection as Spring coaxes forth fecundity in the dark soil of Holy Saturday and the tragic beauty of Holy Week.

CHAPTER SEVEN

EASTER: LOVE WINS

I n the year of the pandemic, our congregation's Easter Service was held
on Zoom. We began the service with
"Christ the Lord is Risen Today" trying
to sing it in unison. As we proclaimed God's victory over death,
we discovered the auditory chaos built into Zoom when a whole
congregation sings in unison, with the loudest voices taking center
stage. Our Zoom singing was so cacophonous, I was tempted to
stop the music. But our congregation soldiered on, realizing that
authentic worship is always live, sometimes disorganized, often
disruptive, and a vehicle of spiritual transformation and healing
amid our congregational messiness.

Easter like Christmas suffers from being too well known, and
too theologically domesticated. The resurrection is something we
are expected to believe, without any questions or doubts, despite its
defiance of logic and law. Church-going Christians have heard the
stories dozens of times so that for many of us they have lost their
edge. We know there will be a happy ending and take resurrection
for granted. We cruise from Palm Sunday to Easter, assuming Jesus
was in full control, certain of what was to come, and thus saw
the crucifixion and death as mere inconveniences for the Eternal
Word. Gnostic denial of Jesus' suffering is always a temptation
for those too familiar with the resurrection story. Jesus' followers
never expected a resurrection until their encounters with the Living Jesus transformed their depression and despair to ecstasy and
empowerment. The encounters with the Resurrected One provoke
amazement and surprise. Like our congregation's Easter singing, the
resurrection stories, along with the Christmas stories, reflect many
voices and perspectives. The early Christian movement, including
those who created the New Testament canon, was content with
mystery and diversity in understanding this world-changing event.

Today, we need to include memories of lament, grief, and divine absence in our resurrection celebrations. The joy of Easter is hollow without the conflict of Thursday, the agony of Friday, and the silence of Saturday.

We can no more articulate the mechanics of resurrection than we can describe Jesus' birth or the physiology and energetic power of Jesus' healing ministry. The only possible earthly witness, Jesus, does not share the details of his resurrection experience. We don't know what Jesus experienced in the interim between Good Friday and Easter morning. Was Jesus in a deep sleep, resting dreamlessly in the bosom of Abraham? Was he fully attuned with the Divine Parent, experiencing the bliss of complete unity and unobstructed communication? Did he somehow rise to Sonship in its fullness, fully spirit, and fully present to the universe, before once again returning to the body? Did he as the Epistle of Peter suggest minister to those who died prior to the resurrection, awakening to their deeper identity and the opportunity to live abundantly? The gospels give us no information on these pivotal moments, just as they are silent about Jesus' lost years between twelve and thirty. While we don't hear anything of Jesus' inner life in the season following his resurrection, the events of the forty days between Easter and the Ascension give us a clue to Jesus' mission and our own twenty-first-century calling.

FORTY DAYS OF RESURRECTION

Christ is alive! Jesus lives! The resurrection encounters, however, we understand them, transform despair to mission among Jesus' first followers. The fearful become faithful. The passive become passionate. The tomb becomes the womb of amazing possibilities. Something happened that changed everything. Perhaps a "deeper magic," as C.S. Lewis says in *The Lion, The Witch, and the Wardrobe,* resurrects Jesus and his followers, an encounter with the Real yet indescribable wonders of God's Love. Beyond the rational mind, or our current awareness, are deeper and higher dimensions of reality, seldom experienced, but known by mystics, shamans, medicine persons, and sages. The Energy of Love changes souls and cells, and bursts forth in life, busting open the tomb and opening the future.

Like gospel accounts of Jesus' life, we catch just a glimpse of the forty-day period between Easter and the Ascension. There is no attempt among the gospel writers or those who created the New Testament canon to give a uniform story, and the diversity of stories in some ways adds to their credibility. The resurrected Jesus was experienced in different ways and chose to appear in varied ways to his followers. Initially, only those for whom the doors of perception were opened experienced the resurrection. This is still true today insofar as the life-transforming Jesus must leap beyond the abstractions and existential distance of the page to a personal experience to truly know him. We discover the Living Jesus on the pathway in our prayer life, daily encounters, and prophetic challenges. Still, the resurrection encounters help us experience the living Christ and learn to "practice resurrection" in our time and place just as Jesus taught resurrection practices to his followers.

MARY OF MAGDALA AND HER COMPANIONS

"Who will roll away the stone for us from the entrance of the tomb?" Mary of Magdala and her friends ask. (Mark 16:3) They are in despair, realistically recognizing their inability to share one last act of love with their teacher and friend until they encounter the empty tomb and experience an open future. There is no encounter with the Risen Jesus in the original texts of Mark's gospel. There is only the promise that they will see Jesus and the command to tell the male disciples. While the longer ending to Mark, added at a later time, points to encounters with Jesus and his first followers, there is something evocative about the empty tomb as primary witness, suggesting that we don't need the whole story to affirm the life-changing power of Jesus. Faith opens the door to deeper perceptions and new ways of seeing reality. Others' stories, whether angelic in the case of Mark's extended gospel or shared in our families or faith communities, awaken the provocative possibility that the One we follow will always be a mystery, never pinned down by church or doctrine, but providing us with more than we can ask and imagine when we follow his path.

Mary of Magdala takes center stage in the first sightings of Jesus. While Mary of Magdala and the "other Mary" encounter Jesus on their way back to the disciples, Mary of Magdala's meeting with Jesus in the Garden provides a pattern for a way Jesus may reveal himself to us. In Matthew's version, Jesus tells the two Mary's, "Do not be afraid; go and tell my brothers to go to Galilee; there they will see me." (Matthew 28:10) Jesus comes to us in our fear and anxiety, whether it relates to the pandemic, national chaos, our mortality, or our quest for justice, and calms our fears and gives us a mission and the energy and insight to live out the calling we've received, "Go and tell, share the good news, be amazed and inspired, I am alive in the world."

In the Garden, Mary mistakes her friend and teacher for the gardener. Distraught, she is unable to recognize Jesus until he calls her name, "Mary." Jesus comes to us in many ways – through the teachings of our church, scripture, others' witnesses, and mystical experiences. Life-changing encounters are always concrete and first-person. Jesus calls our name, addressing us uniquely in our unique life situation. While we may have a personal relationship with Jesus, ultimately Jesus has a personal relationship with us, providing us with the insights, challenge, comfort, and wisdom we need for our concrete, embodied, and historical lives. Called by name, we may want to limit Jesus to the way we have encountered him in our community, scripture, and religious experience. But Jesus – like the Holy Spirit - is unfettered by doctrine and institution. Mary wants to hold onto Jesus, but he cautions her that he is no longer limited by his physical presence or the way she has known him in the past. In "ascending to the Father," Jesus is going global. His revelation and presence from now on will be both personal and planetary, inspiring us individually and in our communities, yet actively seeking wholeness in every culture and human condition.

ON THE ROAD AND IN THE HOUSE

My closest spiritual friend once gave me a crystal paperweight with the inscription, *Solvitur Ambulando*, "it will be solved in the walking." She knew that my daily sunrise beach walks were the most creative, prayerful, and inspirational times of the day for me. Many of the insights in this text came as gifts from the Spirit as I was along Craigville or Covell's Beaches or through the picturesque village of Craigville. When our bodies move, our spirits do as well. Each moment provides a new vista and a new pathway to spiritual, intellectual, or relational adventure.

Jesus is on the road. He joins two followers who are perplexed by the events of Easter morning. They have the women's witness but are struggling to believe the amazing angelic message, "Jesus lives." As they saunter along, Jesus the rabbi unfolds the biblical message, revealing deeper truths of scripture manifest in the events of the past few days. After several miles of walking, they arrive at the village of Emmaus and despite their emotional weariness, they invite Jesus to join them for supper. When Jesus breaks the bread, their eyes were opened and they now know that they have been entertaining the Risen Jesus, the Messiah and Healer. Immediately, Jesus vanishes from their sight. (Luke 24:13-35)

While we don't need to worry about chronology consistency in the Easter stories, it is clear that the Risen One is on the move, wishing to reveal himself, comforting the fearful and illuminating the questioning. On the road to Emmaus, Jesus begins forty days of teaching and spiritual formation. We only get a few accounts of Jesus' encounters with his first followers but we can expect that just as the Spirit guides and tutors us, Jesus taught his followers, perhaps even giving them healing techniques, as he prepared them for the greater things they would be doing as they assumed their vocation of sharing the gospel with the whole world. Emmaus is everywhere, as Marcus Borg suggests, when we discover Jesus alongside us and experience him in shared meals, inspirational conversations, and loving encounters.

In these forty days, Jesus continued his mission as spirit-person, healer, wisdom giver, and movement maker, to use the conceptuality of Marcus Borg. In the unity of the pre-and-post resurrection stories, Jesus prepared his followers for the adventures ahead. John's Gospel rightly reminds us that we cannot encompass Jesus' ministry when he notes that "there were many other things that Jesus did." (John 21:25) Jesus cannot be frozen in place, encompassed by our doctrines, or controlled by our institutions. Like God's Spirit, the wind of Christ goes "where it chooses, and you hear the sound of it, but you do not know where it comes from or where it goes." (John 3:8) As soon as his followers' hearts are warmed at the Emmaus dinner table, Jesus vanishes, off to share resurrection spirit with another group of followers, and challenging us to be like the wind as well, grounded in the Spirit, yet unfettered in faith and practice. (John 3:8)

Breathing Space

"And Jesus breathed on them, and said to them, 'Receive the Holy Spirit.'" Sheltering in place as many of us were in the time of pandemic, the disciples receive Jesus' healing and empowering Spirit. We can't fully fathom Jesus' resurrection body. On the one hand, his body was recognizable. He was known by his physical appearance and his Calvary wounds. On the other hand, he could teleport from place to place, unhindered by the limitations of space and time. His spiritual body, though incarnational in nature, was also able to go through walls. Could Jesus have had some sort of highly charged quantum body, more highly energetic than our own? Could the energy of the universe, the power of the big bang, be coursing through Jesus' resurrection body? Could the power energizing Jesus' healing ministry have been transformed to the cellular level enabling him to defy the "gross" patterns of physical resistance and location? Could his body have been a living prayer, nonlocal and ubiquitous?

Jesus gives his followers spiritual resuscitation. He enlivens and energizes them and gives them his peace. Yet, the peace that Jesus gives is an active, restless, peace. They are to go out in the world and not remain in the upper room. They are to become prophets and spiritual teachers of a new age and co-creators of a new world. Alfred North Whitehead describes peace in terms of a widening of interest which joins our care for ourselves with our care for others. This widening of interest is the stature that enables us to embrace our own well-being and fulfillment with others' well-being and fulfillment. Peace awakens us to the graceful and sometimes challenging interdependence of life which inspires us to go from self-interest and congregational and national affirmation to world loyalty.

In that moment of peace-filled spiritual resuscitation, Jesus empowers his followers to represent him on earth, not in a punitive way, although their work will embody his challenge to seek justice and walk humbly with God, but in a way that promotes healing and wholeness for all persons and nations.

In that upper room, did Jesus begin to teach his followers "advanced" techniques of spiritual transformation and healing that came to fruition in the early Christian movement, described in Acts of the Apostles? As a reiki teacher-master, I use certain attunement processes to raise persons' spiritual and healing energy. Could Jesus have done likewise, in a way dwarfs the reiki initiations I employ? Could Jesus' breath have been the wind of creation, that blew over the waters setting in motion the physical, moral, and spiritual arcs of historical evolution? (Genesis 1:1-5) Could Jesus have provided "practices" of resurrection living, enabling them to transform cells as well as souls and share Jesus' mystical experience with others? This is all speculative, but Jesus promised that his followers would receive "power from on high" and the "baptism of the Spirit." (Luke 24:49; Acts 1:5) Could this divine breathing have opened up Jesus' followers' spiritual energy centers in preparation for the Pentecost Spirit?

FROM DOUBT TO AFFIRMATION.

Thomas is one of my spiritual heroes despite being the butt of many simplistic and unnuanced sermons, chiding him for his lack of faith. Of course, Thomas is not alone in his doubts about the resurrection. Luke notes that the disciples responded to Mary of Magdalene and her friends' ecstatic report of Jesus' resurrection with incredulity, "these words seemed to them an idle tale, and they did not believe them." (Luke 24:11)

In John's account of Thomas' doubt, Jesus appears to come and go as he pleases. After the life-transforming spiritual resuscitation on Easter night, he absents himself for several days. During that time, Thomas returns to his friends, hears the amazing news of resurrection, but needs to be sure before he embraces the new reality of resurrection. Of a philosophical and analytic perspective, Thomas asserts that "unless I see the mark of the nails in his hands, and put my finger in the mark of the nails, and my hand in his side, I will not believe." (John 20:25) He wants to base his faith on the solid ground of experience, not just the testimony of others.

How excruciating that week must have been for Thomas. He was the only one out of the resurrection loop. The other disciples were living in resurrection amazement, while he lived with the void of uncertainty. Yet, the amazing thing is that Thomas remained. He lived with the discomfort and questioning for a week, hopeful that his questions and prayers would be answered.

I appreciate Thomas' doubt and see him as a model and not a caution in the life of faith. When I was in college, I wondered if I could remain a Christian. Raised in a conservative Baptist home, my faith began to waver in junior high and, doctrinally speaking, had collapsed by high school. I could no longer believe what I had been taught as a child and teen. I found my spiritual solace in American Transcendentalism and Asian religions. But, in college,

I found Paul Tillich's *Dynamics of Faith* and discovered that doubt was not a sign of unbelief but a witness to the seriousness with which a person took their faith. I realized that as long as Jesus was important to me, and that the way of Jesus mattered, I could call myself a Christian. Like author Madeleine L'Engle, I learned that I could believe with all my doubts.

When Thomas finally encounters the Risen Jesus, he experiences God's peace, and proclaims "My Lord and my God!" He had seen the Living Jesus and found his own life mission. The mystery remains: how can the Risen Jesus have a corporeal and wounded body and yet be able to appear and disappear at will, and physically enter locked rooms? But that was beside the point. Thomas had experienced the Risen, Wounded One, and was propelled to global ministry.

During my years as Protestant University Chaplain at Georgetown University, I had a congregant of Indian descent whose last name was "Samuel." When I enquired about the origin of her name, commenting that it didn't sound Indian to me, she responded that her family was from a long line of Thomas Christians. Thomas the doubter was also Thomas the pilgrim and evangelist, who journeyed across today's Iran, Afghanistan, and Pakistan into India where he preached the good news of God's salvation in Jesus Christ. Perhaps, Thomas alone of the original followers had the intellectual and spiritual bandwidth to dialogue with Hindu and rishis and Buddhist monks, listening to their metaphysical visions and sharing the Word and Wisdom God incarnate in Jesus Christ. In encountering the Risen Jesus, Thomas grew in spiritual stature and discovered that from honest doubt comes deep belief, sufficient to propel him beyond the Jewish-Roman world to the shores of the Ganges.

LORD, YOU HAVE COME TO SEASHORE

On the seashore, Jesus cooks breakfast for seven disciples. (John 21:1-14) Once again, the embodied Christ not only can intuit where a shoal of fish is to be found but also knows how to make a tasty meal. The Risen One is fully incarnate and proves his physical reality by eating a piece of fish. (Luke 24:42-43) The world is saved one act and person at a time. No great teaching or act of power, but divinity in the simple acts of cooking and eating. Every moment bears divine impression. Resurrection can be practiced as we do ordinary things with loving hands and hearts. As W.H. Auden concludes his Christmas oratorio, *For the Time Being*

> He is the Way.
> Follow Him through the Land of Unlikeness;
> You will see rare beasts, and have unique adventures.
> He is the Truth.
> Seek Him in the Kingdom of Anxiety;
> You will come to a great city
>   that has expected your return for years.
> He is the Life.
> Love Him in the World of the Flesh;
> And at your marriage all its occasions shall dance for joy.

BEYOND FAILURE, MISSION!

No doubt Peter felt uneasy as he encountered the Risen Jesus. His protest of loyalty, even to death, and his abandonment and denial were an unbearable burden. Perhaps knowing Peter is unable to make amends, Jesus reaches out, giving Peter one more opportunity to become the Rock he is destined to be. Jesus practices the gentle and subtle, and yet piercing, art of spiritual formation. He is Peter's *anamcara*, the friend of his soul, who calls him to deeper love and loyalty. Love beyond betrayal and failure. Love that resurrects our deadened spirits and breathes new energy into our lives, so that we can face our deepest fears, including the fear of incapacity, with God as our companion. Perhaps, Jesus remembers his own agony on the cross when he says to Peter, "when you grow old, you will stretch out your hands, and someone else will fasten a belt around you and take you where you do not wish to go." (John 21:9) As early church theologians proclaimed, by living through every season of life, Jesus made every moment of life from conception to death holy.

Jesus experienced the holiness of weakness and vulnerability on the cross. Jesus carried the pain of the world, the weight of torture, trauma, pain, abandonment, fear, on Calvary. No substitutionary atonement, appeasing an angry and score-keeping God, Jesus feels our pain and transforms pain into trust and compassion. Now pushing seventy, I am daily aware of my mortality. As a generally healthy person, who nevertheless has age-related risk factors, I have experienced a degree of fear and trembling during the time of pandemic. I worry that someday I will be taken where I don't want to go and that I may lose my agency and independence and have to depend on the kindness of strangers. I need Jesus' real presence and to know that:

> We do not live to ourselves, and we do not die to ourselves. If we live, we live to the Lord, we die to the Lord; so then, whether we live or whether we die, we are the Lord's. For to this end Christ died and lived again, so that he might be Lord of both the dead and the living. (Romans 14:7-9)

As a song of my childhood promises, "Jesus knows our every weakness, take it to the Lord in prayer."

ON EARTH AS IT IS IN HEAVEN

The departure of Jesus is equally mysterious. Forty days after the resurrection, Jesus ascends into the heavens. The story of the Ascension is, to some degree, mythical, describing a three-story universe that is unbelievable, if taken literally. What seems to be happening in the Ascension is Jesus' turning over of his mission to his followers. Though I wonder why Jesus had to leave us, and how much more good he would have done had he stayed (after all, he has eternal life!), I realize that in order for his followers to grow to their full potential, Jesus – like a loving parent – had to give them space to grow. No helicopter parent, God encourages freedom, creativity, and loving interdependence, balancing our initiative and independence with our responsibilities to one another. As they gaze to the heavens, transfixed by the ascending Jesus, angelic guides tell Jesus' followers, "Men of Galilee, why you stand looking up at heaven?" The future of God's reign on earth is in our hands. God calls and the response is ours. Though our spiritual treasures are fallible, earthen vessels, we are God's hands and feet, as Teresa of Avila counsels. Though we can do nothing without God's all-embracing love, God needs us to heal the world. Though the odds appear against us in our time of protest, pandemic, and climate change, we have the promise that God is with us, inspiring, challenging, and comforting, promising "lo, I am with you always, to the end of the age." (Matthew 28:20) Fortified by God's resurrection love, we can practice resurrection, claiming our place as God's companions in healing the world.

CHAPTER EIGHT

PENTECOST: UNFETTERED SPIRIT

Pentecost describes the spiritual unfolding of the Jesus movement from Jerusalem to the whole earth. While the embodied Jesus plays only a small role in the Pentecostal vision of Acts of the Apostles, Jesus is the motive force in the expanding spiritual and moral arc of history. The unfettered and restless Spirit of Pentecost is the Spirit of Jesus freed from the constraints of locality and now universal in scope. Jesus epitomizes the humorous quip, "God is like Elvis, you see God everywhere." Wherever there is Spirit, there is Jesus. As the Jesus movement expands, Jesus' ministry of hospitality transcends Jew or Greek, slave or free, male or female, old or young, wise and unlearned, and every binary division humans try to erect. Today the moral and spiritual arc of Jesus challenges those who follow the Resurrected One to break down every fetter, whether it applies to citizenship, sexuality, or race. The Pentecost season invites us to recognize that whatever we do unto others, we are doing unto Jesus.

In the Pentecost season, the gifts of Christ become our gifts. There is enough Jesus to go around for all of us! We are the ones that God is waiting for now. We can be as Gandhi counsels, the change we want to see in the world. We are God's hands and feet. Empowered by the Spirit of Christ, with the Holy Spirit as our guide, challenge, and comfort, the energy of love embodied in the unity of Jesus with the Divine Parent courses through us.

> "Do you not believe that I am in the Father and the Father is in me? The words that I say to you I do not speak on my own; but the Father who dwells in me does his works. Believe me that I am in the Father and the Father is in me; but if you do not, then believe me because of the works themselves. Very

truly, I tell you, the one who believes in me will also do the
works that I do and, in fact, will do greater works than these,
because I am going to the Father. I will do whatever you
ask in my name, so that the Father may be glorified in the
Son. If in my name you ask me for anything, I will do it."
(John 14:10-14)

Jesus promises that those who follow his way will become the
body of Christ, interdependent and creative, joining the personal
and the planetary, and individual achievement and the common
good. We will become the spirit persons, prophetic healers, movement makers, and living parables and wisdom teachers in our time.
When the energy of the vine of Christ flows through us, we will
bear much fruit and become agents in personal and global transformation, incarnating the promise of Ephesians 3:18-21.

> I pray that you may have the power to comprehend,
> with all the saints, what is the breadth and length and height
> and depth, and to know the love of Christ that surpasses
> knowledge, so that you may be filled with all the fullness of
> God. Now to him who by the power at work within us is
> able to accomplish abundantly far more than all we can ask or
> imagine, to him be glory in the church and in Christ Jesus to
> all generations, forever and ever.

The historical Jesus lives on, not bound by place and time, but
present in every movement of healing and reconciliation. Jesus the
Christ is everywhere. God's prophetic energy of love, embodied
and living on in Jesus' Spirit and the community that bears his
name, challenges everything that stands in the way of abundant
living. (John 10:10) In this current time of protest and pandemic,
my image of the living Jesus, cutting across time, place, and person
and yet responding personally to each of us, drew me to the final
speech of Tom Joad from John Steinback's *Grapes of Wrath*.

> I'll be aroun' in the dark. I'll be everywhere-wherever you
> look. Wherever there is a fight so hungry people can eat, I'll be
> there. Wherever there is a cop beatin' up a guy, I'll be there...I'll

be in the way kids laugh when they're hungry and they know supper's ready. An' when our folk eat the stuff they raise an' live in the houses they build—why, I'll be there.[17]

ENCOUNTERING THE LIVING JESUS

The resurrected Christ moves through persons' lives in the first century and in our time, inspiring us to widen our circles of trust, community, and hospitality. Whenever we encounter Jesus, we receive assurance and a mission. Our attentiveness to the way of Jesus enables us to be Jesus' incarnations in our own personal and communal adventures. Acts of the Apostles describes three pivotal encounters with the Living Jesus. These post-Ascension mystical encounters are intended to remind us that the Spirit of Jesus lives on, inspiring, challenging, empowering, and sometimes surprising us. Indeed, the book of Acts is an account of the animated and inspired body of Christ, the ongoing adventures of the Risen Jesus in our world of tragic beauty and amazing wonder and chaos.

THE DEATH OF STEPHEN

Faithful to the gospel message, Stephen is arrested and sentenced to death by stoning. (Acts 5:54-60) As he is being convicted, Stephen has a mystical experience in which he:

> gazed into heaven and saw the glory of God and Jesus standing at the right hand of God. "Look," he said, "I see the heavens opened and the Son of Man standing at the right hand of God."

Even as the stones strike him, Stephen looks beyond persecution and death to companionship with the Living Jesus as he prays, "Lord Jesus, receive my spirit." In the spirit of his savior and teacher, Stephen knelt down and prayed, "Lord, do not hold this sin against them."

---

17 John Steinbeck, *The Grapes of Wrath* (New York: Penguin Books, 2006), *419.*

Stephen's mystical experience may be a dramatic example of the call and response characterizing every moment of our lives. God reaches out to the martyred disciple, providing him a vision of God's intimate presence and Stephen's personal destiny. Inspired and empowered by God, Stephen opens to divine inspiration which cleanses the doors of perception, enabling him to feel God's presence and respond by choosing to become an agent of healing and forgiveness.

PAUL'S NEW ROAD.

The Living Jesus reaches out to the persecuting Paul. On his way to Damascus to arrest followers of Jesus, Paul has a God-given mystical experience that entirely changes his life's mission.

> Now as he was going along and approaching Damascus, suddenly a light from heaven flashed around him. He fell to the ground and heard a voice saying to him, "Saul, Saul, why do you persecute me?" He asked, "Who are you, Lord?" The reply came, "I am Jesus, whom you are persecuting. But get up and enter the city, and you will be told what you are to do." The men who were traveling with him stood speechless because they heard the voice but saw no one. Saul got up from the ground, and though his eyes were open, he could see nothing; so they led him by the hand and brought him into Damascus. For three days he was without sight, and neither ate nor drank. (Acts 9:3-9)

Jesus also appears to a disciple in Damascus, Ananias, assuring him that Paul has been transformed from enemy to friend, and that he is to be Paul's mentor and spiritual guide, helping him become mature in his faith and mission to the Gentiles. Mysticism leads to mission for both Paul and Ananias. The pre-and-post resurrection Jesus enlightens us and then gives us a lifetime vocation. In Paul's case, mysticism leads to ministry to the Gentile world and expanding the Christian movement to go beyond ethnicity to become a global movement. What is unique about these mystical encounters is that they are initiated by Jesus. Jesus comes to us, addressing us in terms of our life situations, previous history, limitations, and possibilities, and lures us forward to world-transforming mission. The divine call comes in each moment of experience, and all authentic call experiences are congruent with Christ's Spirit moving in the world. Still, some moments, such as these described in Acts of the Apostles, are more definitive of Jesus' mission and explicitly call us toward living out our vocation in the way of Jesus.

AN EXPANDING GOSPEL.

Jesus doesn't directly appear in the mystical experiences of Peter and Cornelius (Acts 10:1-48). Peter's vision of the smorgasbord of unclean foods – no doubt, some of our Cape Cod delicacies such as crab, clams, and lobsters – is an invitation to a global spirituality. Jesus' common table is going global, excluding no one. In the synchronicity of Spirit, Cornelius also experiences divine inspiration, in this case, to reach out to Peter. Breaking barriers of ethnicity and lifestyle, Peter crosses Cornelius' threshold and all heaven breaks loose. Ecstasy overcomes ethnicity as God's Spirit inspires outsiders to praise. All that is left is to baptize them "in the name of Jesus Christ." Once at the margins, they are now at the center of the emerging Jesus movement.

Pentecost is the season of surprising spiritual transformation. The living Jesus enables us to cross boundaries, do great and wondrous things, heal the sick of body, mind, and spirit, mend broken relationships, face death with courage and hope, and share good news to the whole world. Although he is not physically present, the spiritual energy of Jesus inspires and transfigures. Christ is alive and we become his hands, feet, and voices – the healers, wisdom teachers, prophets, movement makers and spirit persons for our tenuous and traumatic times.

LIVING IN THE SPIRIT

As a first-year college student, I returned to church. After leaving church in high school, I had traveled on the magical mystery tour, imbibed in the summer of love, and explored the spirituality of Buddha and the Hindu rishis. I was on a quest for God and found God in unlikely places but was looking for something more – a community of seekers who humbly sought to be faithful to the way of Jesus. My return to church, ironically, occurred a week after learning Transcendental Meditation, at a former fraternity house, now ashram in Berkeley, California. Returning to church, I was greeted, accepted, and then given a task by the two pastors of Grace Baptist Church, John Akers and George L. "Shorty" Collins, whose nickname was ironic, given his 6-foot-7-inch stature.

At Grace Baptist Church, I learned that faith was a matter of lifestyle rather than orthodoxy. Heaven was to be experienced on earth as we sought the peaceable realm in opposing the Vietnam War, supporting Cesar Chavez United Farm Workers, and responding to the needs of the homeless. The environmental movement was just emerging and we were learning that we needed to live simply to ensure planetary survival. John Akers often spoke of "living in the style of Jesus," which meant constantly seeking to live as Jesus did in the complexities of the 1970s.

The first followers of Jesus sought to embody Jesus' Spirit, the values and lifestyle of Jesus, in the emerging Christian movement. Metanoia, or repentance, was at the heart of their personal and communal spirituality, and our own spiritual quests today. Then and now, we are challenged to make a U-turn away from injustice and head to the far horizons of God's Shalom. In words coined by Paul, they sought to go beyond the world's mold by constant transformation. (Romans 12:2) They sought to incarnate Jesus' all-embracing love in lives of transformational discipleship, seeking to be open to constant conversion, growth, and companionship with the Spirit of Christ in the hands, feet, and hearts. This led to the emergence of a new kind of community, profoundly countercultural in its embodiment of Jesus' Galilean ministry. A community without walls and boundaries, in which God was a circle – or perhaps a spiral, whose center was everywhere, embracing each creature as beloved, and whose circumference was nowhere, embracing the whole earth in its diversity as God's beloved community.

Just as Jesus was the fulfillment, though not negation, of the prophetic vision, embodied in space and time, the early Christian movement began to see itself as the body of Christ, animated and inspired by the Holy Spirit. In the spirit of Jesus' all-embracing call to discipleship, the church of the Pentecost saw divine inspiration as both global and intimate:

> the last days it will be, God declares,
> that I will pour out my Spirit upon all flesh,
> and your sons and your daughters shall prophesy,
> and your young men shall see visions,
> and your old men shall dream dreams.
> Even upon my slaves, both men and women,
> in those days I will pour out my Spirit;
>   and they shall prophesy. (Acts 2:17-18)

As Jesus opened his table to everyone, "eating with tax collectors and sinners," the Christian movement embodied a common table and aspired to economic structures that embraced everyone in the community. These fledgling communities became the body of Christ, incarnating the Risen One in day-to-day acts of mercy and inclusion. They became, and in some places, remain Christ's messy incarnation in the ambiguities and conflicts of personal, community, and planetary history.

> Awe came upon everyone, because many wonders and signs were being done by the apostles. All who believed were together and had all things in common; they would sell their possessions and goods and distribute the proceeds to all, as any had need. Day by day, as they spent much time together in the temple, they broke bread at home and ate their food with glad

and generous[1] hearts, praising God and having the goodwill of all the people. And day by day the Lord added to their number those who were being saved. (Acts 2:42-47)

The mysticism of Pentecost led to mission and transformed minds led to transformation of culinary, domestic, and financial practices. As Jesus proclaimed God's realm "on earth as it is in heaven," Jesus' first followers sought to live out what the Risen Jesus had announced. With the "spirit of Lord" upon them as it had animated Jesus, they experienced God's Shalom, the Jubilee Year of relational and economic healing, emerging in common tables, healing ministry, and inclusive hospitality. Cells and souls were transformed in the Jesus movement just as they had been transformed in Jesus' ministry of healing of body, mind, spirit, and social location.

Living in the style of Jesus meant being the embodiment of Christ in the world through hospitality, healing, and holistic spirituality. Pentecostal hospitality incarnated Jesus' boundary-breaking and ever-widening circle of salvation, dissolving boundaries through table fellowship and worship. Like Jesus, the early Christian movement grew in wisdom and stature, beginning first with the incarnation of hospitality toward the Jewish community in all its diversity and later experiencing the growing pains of welcoming all, Gentile, marginalized, enslaved, unclean, and sinful into God's community of love. It was messy, trying to move from a Jewish sect to an inclusive movement, but in the messiness was grace, healing, and creative transformation.

Signs and wonders reflected Jesus' healing ministry, the energy of love that restored and enlivened cells, souls, and relationships. As Jesus touched and made whole, using words, energy, welcome, and inspiration, the early Christian movement addressed the whole person, recognizing that salvation or wholeness began in the here and now. We don't need to wait until we die to experience resurrection. Abundant life is right earth on earth as it will be in heaven

All were invited to become spirit persons, enjoying the fruits of salvation in this present lifetime. Salvation is seamless and all-inclusive. Just as Jesus invited his followers to become more than could imagine and to discover their gifts for mission, the early Christian community became a laboratory for spiritual transformation, a living spiritual body, aiming to nurture each member's gifts for the common good and personal wholeness. In the spirit of Jesus' parable of the lost sheep, these early communities saw themselves as embodiments of God's incarnational love in Jesus. All persons were holy and all places holy ground. God's vision of Shalom inspired care for the least of these, grounded in the recognition that salvation is communal as well as personal and that the ninety-nine remain incomplete until the hundredth finds wholeness. Rooted in the mysticism of the prophets and later embodied in the Jewish mysticism of the Kabbalah, the early church knew the meaning of the rabbinical exhortation: "Whoever destroys a single soul should be considered the same as one who has destroyed a whole world. And whoever saves one single soul should be considered the same as one who has saved a whole world."[18]

Living in the style of Jesus, the early Christian movement shared in his messy incarnation, embedded in the ambiguities of history, experiencing its own struggles and growing pains, charting a countercultural course, and for a brief moment, living without the benefit of political and economic power, seeking to embody God's realm on earth as it is in heaven. Making it up as it went along, inspired by a spirit free – at least for a moment – of doctrinal and ritualistic orthodoxy, these apprentice spirit persons, like their Savior and Teacher, ranged the earth planting seeds of wholeness and welcome to stranger and friend alike. Christ was alive and known in the breaking bread, healing touch, loving word, and welcome embrace. That is still our calling as Pentecost people: to plant seeds of grace, healing, and transformation, to heal the sick, welcome the marginalize, and seek a world where all are pilgrims and none are strangers.

---

18 Abraham Joshua Heschel, *The Prophets*, volume one (Peabody, MA: Hendrickson Publishers, 1962), 14.

CHAPTER NINE

CREATION SEASON: FOR GOD SO LOVED THE WORLD

I grew up listening to Ethel Waters singing "His Eye is on the Sparrow, and I Know He Watches Me" on televised Billy Graham Crusades. As I child immersed in the beauty of small-town America, I took comfort in that hymn. I felt a kinship with nature, with the mustard seeds I planted, walking along the Salinas River with my best friend Richard Jenkins, listening to chirping birds, and feeling the warm California winds against my face.

Growing up in a small-town Baptist church, one of my favorite scriptures came from the Sermon on the Mount:

> Look at the birds of the air; they neither sow nor reap nor gather into barns, and yet your Heavenly Father feeds them... Consider the lilies of the field, how they grow, they neither toil nor spin, yet I tell you even Solomon in all his glory was not clothed like one of these. But if God so clothes the grass of the field, which is alive today and tomorrow is thrown into the oven, will God not much more clothe you – you of little faith? (Matthew 7:26, 28-30)

The Jesus I knew in childhood loved the birds of the air, the lilies of the fields, the ocean waves, and dogs and cats. I have written a number of times about how I became a theologian, questioning the faith of orthodox Christianity, when a prim church lady told me that her dog, with whom I was playing all weekend, would not be going to heaven! I remembered Jesus saying, "Are not two sparrows sold for a penny? Yet not one of them will fall to the ground apart from your Father." (Matthew 10:29)

Jesus never gave an environmentalist sermon, but Jesus loved the earth. Jesus affirmed that "God so loved the world" – the cosmos, not just humankind – that Jesus came to live with us. The Incarnation is the ultimate affirmation of embodiment. The word and wisdom made flesh is just as present in our cells as our souls. Jesus' parables highlighted flora and fauna, vines and seeds, and Jesus saw his own mission in terms of a lively energetic vine whose sap flows into all of us, and whose power in our lives requires our spiritual pruning.

The Incarnation is the ultimate inspiration for what a growing number of Christians celebrate as the Season of Creation, stretching from September 1 to October 4, the Feast of St. Francis. In the context of ecological destruction and global climate change, much of it perpetrated by the marriage of capitalism and consumption with Northern hemisphere Christianity, many Christians believe that we need to affirm God's love for all creation, the value of non-human life, and our calling to be stewards and gardeners of the earth. Like the philosopher Alfred North Whitehead, they believe that aim of the universe is the creation of beauty and that God calls us to be companions in bringing beauty to the earth. God calls us to live simply so that others in the human and non-human world may simply live. God loves the fetus and God also loves the right whale baby, of which there are only four hundred on the planet. God calls us to choose life for all creation, not just ourselves, and to expand our concern from self-interest to world loyalty, extending to countless generations of human and non-human life.

In the first century, humans were still at the mercy of environmental forces more powerful than themselves. While Roman ingenuity was beginning to shape nature for economic, military, and political gain and personal comfort, humankind's impact on the earth was still minimal. The seeds of ecological destruction may have been sown in the Roman Empire, but their pernicious harvest had not yet come to fruition. In the marriage of Platonic and Neo-Platonic asceticism with Christian theology, focus on heaven and immortality replaced the Hebraic immersion in embodiment in both human and non-human life. Spiritualized images of survival after death and resurrection drew people away from the joys of creation to focus on the ecstasy of disembodied immortality. In monastic circles turning from the body and its pleasures was viewed as necessary for those who wished to have an intimate relationship with God. The binary separation of heaven and earth and spirit and body became the norm in preaching and practical Christianity. The ethics of God's realm "on earth as it is in heaven" was supplanted by Constantinian authoritarianism and a spirituality that encouraged obedience to authorities and the conflation of church and state as a prerequisite for heavenly bliss. The prophetic edge was lost, deadened by power brokers who saw obedience to rulers and perpetuation of the status quo as central to achieving eternal life. From this patriarchal and monarchical perspective, where salvation is a matter of transactional belief and good behavior, there is no need to transform the world if heaven is your destination. In a totally dispirited world, good Christians can champion eco-destruction with chants of "drill, baby, drill."

In contrast, Jesus proclaimed the unity of body, mind, spirit, and relationships in his table fellowship and healing ministry. Jesus' first miracle, transforming water into wine, affirmed the joy of marriage and sexuality and the importance of celebration. Jesus so enjoyed his fellowship with his followers that he earned the dubious reputation as a prophetic party animal. "The son of man came eating and drinking, and they say, 'Look, a glutton and a drunkard, a friend of tax collectors and sinners. Yet wisdom is vindicated by her deeds." (Matthew 11:19) There was a time for Lenten fasting; there was also a time for celebrative partying!

Imagine healing by partying! But also imagine healing by including. Healing through touching the forgotten and lost, the ostracized and spiritually abused. Imagine a touch that releases God's healing energies that transform cells and souls and join us with the human and non-human world in all their amazing diversity.

In the intricate interdependence of life, Jesus felt a profound intimacy with the natural, non-human world. Jesus' intuitive sense of God's presence in the elements of nature enabled Jesus to calm a storm and walk on water. The same intimacy with cells, atoms, and souls was at the heart of his healing ministry, his ability to bring order to disordered spirits, bodies, and natural phenomena. Jesus' "miracles," whether they were social, psychological, physical, or involved forces of nature like storms were naturalistic, expressing his affinity with the embodied world and his energy of love that touched the winds and waves as well as spirits and cells.

Jesus embraced the fullness of the Hebraic spiritual tradition. We know he invoked Psalm 22, "my God, my God, why have you forsaken me," on the cross. We can imagine that in addition to the prophetic writings and the scriptures of law and liberation, Jesus embraced the robust and full-bodied spirituality of the Psalms. Perhaps, he reveled in the world of praise, described in Psalms 148 and 150.

Praise the LORD!
Praise the LORD from the heavens;
praise him in the heights!
Praise him, all his angels;
praise him, all his host!
Praise him, sun and moon;
praise him, all you shining stars!
Praise him, you highest heavens,
and you waters above the heavens!
Let them praise the name of the LORD,
for he commanded and they were created.
He established them forever and ever;
he fixed their bounds, which cannot be passed.
Praise the LORD from the earth,
you sea monsters and all deeps,
fire and hail, snow and frost,
stormy wind fulfilling his command!

Mountains and all hills,
fruit trees and all cedars!
Wild animals and all cattle,
creeping things and flying birds!
Kings of the earth and all peoples,
princes and all rulers of the earth!
Young men and women alike,
old and young together!
Let them praise the name of the LORD,
for his name alone is exalted;
his glory is above earth and heaven…
Let everything that breathes praise God.
(Psalm 148:1-13, Psalm 150:6)

In the Creator's world, "all nature sings and around me rings the music of the spheres."[19] Listening with Jesus to the singing of nature, we are inspired to be God's companions, as I've said before, in healing the earth, not just the human world, but land, sea, sky, and earth, and all that dwells within them. We are God's companions and agents in repairing the creation which gave birth to Jesus.

Incarnation is the ultimate witness to a sacramental universe. The word made flesh is the greatest witness to God's love for our world of human flesh, flora, and fauna and God's mandate that we love the good earth with joyful and passionate care. I conclude this chapter on Jesus' creation spirituality with another hymn from my evangelical childhood in which Jesus walked with me and talked with and told me I was his own child, "Memories of Galilee," from the lips of George Beverly Shea.

Each cooing dove and sighing bough,
That makes the eve so blessed to me,
Has something far diviner now,
It bears me back to Galilee.

---

19   Maltbie Babcock, "This is My Father's World"

Refrain

O Galilee, sweet Galilee,
Where Jesus loved so much to be,
O Galilee, blue Galilee,

Come sing thy song again to me.

Each flowery glen and mossy dell,
Where happy birds in song agree,
Through sunny morn the praises tell
Of sights and sounds in Galilee.

And when I read the thrilling lore
Of Him Who walked upon the sea,
I long, oh, how I long once more
To follow Him in Galilee.[20]

---

20 Robert Morris, "Memories of Galilee."

CHAPTER TEN

THE REALM OF CHRIST: THE ONLY POWER THAT MATTERS

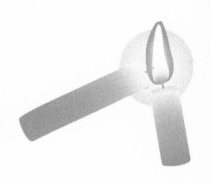

It seems anachronistic to the spirit of this text to focus on Christ the King, or the Realm of Christ Sunday, the last Sunday of the Christian year. Among many persons today, images of sovereignty are typically connected with coercion, exclusion, distancing, and binary thinking. In North American experience, royal mages are often viewed as the most blatant examples of theological social distancing and binary decision-making. From the divine throne, God views our ambiguous world "from a distance," lacking both empathy and intimacy in relation to the challenges we face. While there are many examples of rulers as inspirational and sacrificial, many persons still struggle with the realities of leaders - monarchical, presidential, and pastoral - who wield power coercively, lacking empathy for the vulnerable or persons in their employ. In contrast to negative images of monarchy and sovereignty, messy incarnation affirms relationship and responsiveness as definitive of God's nature. Emmanuel, God with us, is transparent in relating to the world. Jesus shares our joys and sorrows, challenging and comforting real people in real circumstances. Distant and coercive sovereigns deal with abstractions, abstract rules, and threatening edicts. Jesus dealt with concrete situations, thinking globally but living intimately as one of us, experiencing our imperfections, and inspiring us toward wholeness and mission.

Our images of God shape our relationships with one another. Authoritarian and binary images of God inspire authoritarian and divisive relationships, exclusion of otherness, and denunciation of differences. God embedded in the complexities of life models partnership, creativity, openness to diversity, and willingness to embrace new possibilities in relationship to others.

Philosopher Alfred North Whitehead captures the contrast between domineering and relational images of God and the significance of Jesus as an alternative vision of divine activity.

> The notion of God as the 'unmoved mover' is derived from Aristotle, at least so far as Western thought is concerned. The notion of God as 'eminently real' is a favorite doctrine of Christian theology. The combination of the two into the doctrine of an aboriginal, eminently real, transcendent creator, at whose fiat the world came into being, and whose imposed will it obeys, is the fallacy which has infused tragedy into the histories of Christianity and Mahometanism [Islam]. When the Eastern world accepted Christianity, Caesar conquered; and the received text of Western theology was edited by his lawyers. The code of Justinian and the theology of Justinian are two volumes expressing one movement of the human spirit. The brief Galilean vision of humility flickered throughout the ages, uncertainly. In the official formulation of the religion, it has assumed the trivial form of the mere attribution to the Jews image of the Egyptian, Persian, and Roman imperial rulers, which was retained. The Church gave unto God the attributes which belonged exclusively to Caesar...There is, however, in the Galilean origin of Christianity yet another suggestion which does not fit very well with any of the three main strands of thought. It does not emphasize the rule of Caesar, or the ruthless moralist, or the unmoved mover. It dwells upon the tender elements in the world, which slowly and in quietness operate by love.[21]

The Apostle Paul recognized the life-transforming and relational-shaping power of Jesus' messy incarnation in his counsel to the Philippians:

> Let the same mind be in you that was in Christ Jesus,
> who, though he was in the form of God,

---

21   Alfred North Whitehead, *Process and Reality: Corrected Edition* (New York: Press Press, 1978), 342-343.

did not regard equality with God as something to be exploited,
but emptied himself, taking the form of a slave,
being born in human likeness.
And being found in human form,
he humbled himself and became obedient to the point of death—
even death on a cross.
Therefore God also highly exalted him
and gave him the name that is above every name,
so that at the name of Jesus every knee should bend,
   in heaven and on earth and under the earth,
   and every tongue should confess that Jesus Christ is Lord,
   to the glory of God the Father. (Philippians 2:5-11)

Paul's first listeners easily discerned the difference between "Lord Jesus" and "Lord Caesar" just as Jesus' followers and opponents recognized the profound contrast between Jesus' understanding of power and that of the Roman and Jewish leadership. Caesar, Pilate, Herod, and the Temple priesthood rule by fear of punishment, humiliation, death, and excommunication. They executed institutional terror campaigns and police brutality to keep their subjects in line. In relationship to Caesar and his cronies throughout the ages, you bow your knee and confess your loyalty knowing you have no other option if you and your family are to stay alive or escape ostracism and imprisonment. Caesarian rule, whether in Rome or Washington DC, demands adulation, praise, and agreement. Nothing less than absolute loyalty is required in this culture of fear.

The rule of Christ takes a different path. We bow our knees and give praise to Jesus out of gratitude and love, and freedom and not coercion. As the Epistle of John proclaims, "There is no fear in love, but perfect love casts out fear; for fear has to do with punishment, and whoever fears has not reached perfection in love." (I John 4:18) In a similar spirit, Whitehead notes that "if the modern world is to find God, it must find him through love and not fear."[22] While Jesus' way brings abundant life, our creative and fallible quests for

---

22   Alfred North Whitehead, *Religion in the Making*, 73.

wholeness are not punished. Even turning away from God does not diminish God's love but invites a new array of divine possibilities, appropriate to our situation, and reflective of God's care that every lost child find its way home.

On the final Sunday of the Christian liturgy year, followers of Jesus affirm another kind of power, the power of what Thomas Oord describes as "uncontrolling love." Jesus' power is incarnate in healing, hospitality, companionship, and solidarity. For Jesus, power is always guided by love and care for the other's best interests. God is the holy other, not in terms of distance, but in terms of moral and spiritual guidance. Accepting us as we are, God in Christ challenges us to become Christlike. The power of love is the greatest incentive for transformation and the most persuasive inspiration to face our imperfection and failure knowing that Jesus walks beside us, calls our name, and guides us toward new horizons of wholeness and responsibility.

Earlier in this text, I cited process theologian Bernard Loomer's identification of two kinds of power, unilateral power and relational power, which reflect the contrast between Christ and Caesar and authoritarian power and religion and empowering visions of power and faith. As a result of the misuse of power in state and church as well as coercive understandings of God, this discussion bears repeating. Unilateral power is one-directional, coercive, giving but not receiving, acting upon but immune to others' actions. Unilateral power either doesn't or can't experience the pain of others. Unilateral power doubles down, seeing any agency, creativity, or challenge by others as a threat. Living in a zero-sum world, unilateral power, whether divine or human, sees any gains by others as a loss to itself. Accordingly, from this perspective, God must be the all-powerful sovereign, determining every event, or allowing freedom to occur only on God's terms. Creaturely innovation is, by definition, sinful affront to the creator. In contrast, relational power acts but also listens. Relational power elicits the gifts of others, seeking their wellbeing, by responding to their gifts and experiences. Relational power is always growing and sees healthy agency as a source of greater rather than less influence in the world. When we attend to God's vision, responding in our unique way with our own initiative, God's influence is increased in the world. God doesn't determine our future but wants us to be God's hands and feet, creating the future in partnership with God and presenting God with new possibilities for Shalom-seeking in the world.

Unilateral and all-determining power is binary in nature. It separates the world into friend and foe and dehumanizes those who ask questions or hold contrasting viewpoints. Unilateral approaches deny the gifts of the creaturely world. In contrast, the power of a relational God or the relational Jesus has infinite bandwidth, welcoming contrast and diversity and using the challenges of the world as a pathway to achieving just beauty and creative transformation. Again, let us read Bernard Loomer's description of the spiritual stature embodied in Jesus who grew in wisdom and stature, and those who follow their path of ever-widening compassion. This is the stature of God who is the circle whose center is everywhere and whose circumference is nowhere. This is the ever-widening circle of love and understanding we seek as followers of Jesus in politics and personal relationships.

> By size I mean the stature of a person's soul, the range and depth of his love, his capacity for relationships. I mean the volume of life you can take into your being and still maintain your integrity and individuality, the intensity and variety of outlook you can entertain in the unity of your being without feeling defensive or insecure. I mean the strength of your spirit to encourage others to become freer in the development of their diversity and uniqueness.[23]

In all the messiness of life, Jesus is a work, embracing, expanding, and energizing the power of love. Infinitely flexible, not defensively brittle, Jesus constantly widened the circle of love and accepted others' wisdom as a pathway to greater inclusiveness. Whether with persons with leprosy, social outcasts, women, for-

---

23 Bernard Loomer, "S-I-Z-E is the Measure," Harry James Cargas and Bernard Lee, *Religious Experience and Process Theology,* 70

eigners, or tax collectors, Jesus embraced the varieties of human experience, bringing forth beauty where others saw ugliness. As Whitehead says, "God is the poet of the world, with tender patience leading it by his vision of truth, beauty, and goodness."[24]

True power, the power of messy incarnation, redeems the broken, challenges the apathetic, accepts the marginalized, and heals the forgotten, calling all humankind – and this messy planet – to go beyond self-interest and individual privilege to embrace the ever-evolving and always challenging world as God's companions in justice, healing, and love. The is the only power that matters in our messy and beautiful world, the incarnational power of the Loving Jesus.

---

24   Alfred North Whitehead, *Process and Reality,* 346

CHAPTER ELEVEN

THE WORD GOES FORTH: THE EMERGING KINDOM OF JESUS

The scriptures are clear that the gospels only tell a portion of Jesus' ministry. All the books in the known world couldn't contain his words and actions, so says John's Gospel. (John 21:25) Beyond the canonical and extra-canonical ("Gnostic') accounts of Jesus lies the vastness of Jesus' spirituality, teaching, and relationship with the divine. Like the Holy Spirit, Jesus can never be pinned down theologically, ethically, or doctrinally. Still, it is important that we conclude with the word and wisdom of Jesus as it goes forth in history – our history – still shaping us intellectually, ethically, politically, and theologically. The energy and teachings of Jesus go forth across the planet as guideposts for our own spiritual lives, relationships, and political involvement. Jesus' Abba, as John Cobb says, still transforms our lives through our relationship to the words and actions of Jesus the Christ. In this final chapter, we consider the power of Jesus' words to shape our lives two thousand years later. In this brief chapter, I will focus on Jesus' words as they touch our unique time of pluralism, protest, and pandemic, of incivility and environmental crisis. I assume that certain of Jesus' teachings were esoteric and perhaps not found in our written scriptures, that is, reserved for an inner circle as well as public in nature. These are not a matter of disingenuousness on Jesus or the Gospel writers' part, but a recognition that spiritual leaders and teachers address their audience, both individual and communal, concretely in terms of maturity and insight as well as their unique vocations. As a writer, speaker, and spiritual guide, I always speak the truth as I understand it and as others – whether children and laypersons or fellow scholars – can understand it. Jesus' hidden message, congruent with his revealed message, comes to us in times when the spirit speaks to us quietly in sighs too deep for words or in gales of challenge and inspiration.

While scholars and wise laypeople recognize that Jesus' words are remembered and, accordingly, shaped by the concerns and emphases of those who recorded them, the personality and energy of Jesus still shine through. As New Testament scholar and theologian Marcus Borg asserts, we can see in Jesus' life and teaching in terms of five strands, which from my perspective are interdependent and inform one another: spirit person or mystic; healer of body, mind, spirit, and personal and social relationships; wisdom teacher through parables and parabolic actions; social prophet in the line of Amos, Hosea, Micah, and Isaiah; and movement founder whose message goes forth to our time. Jesus is also, as N.T. Wright notes, the pinnacle of the Hebraic prophetic tradition, and the One whose mission in the broadest sense the seventh-century prophets anticipated. Though they did not know the Messiah's identity or chronology or have first-hand insight into the name or techniques of the Expected One, the prophets yearned for someone like Jesus to embody their hopes and dreams. The gospels portray Jesus as the fulfillment and incarnation of the prophetic dream kin-dom of God, the commonwealth of Shalom, in which peace and justice would reign.

While Jesus' vision of God's realm differed from first-century militaristic expectations, he believed that his mission was to proclaim by words and acts, and by his very being, the good news of God's realm in the messiness of our history. Unlike popular unimaginative political expectations, Jesus' realm embraced all creation, going beyond religious, ethnic, and national inclusiveness, and transcended binary divisions of righteous and unrighteous and welcomed and marginalized. In this final chapter, I will present a brief meditation on Jesus' theological perspective, focusing on his parables, relational and ethical teachings, and promises to his followers. I will be sketching a landscape of Jesus' message as I believe it transforms our lives today in the messy maelstrom of our own personal and political histories.

PARABLES OF GOD'S KIN-DOM

Jesus was above all a wisdom teacher, an embodiment of Logos and Sophia in the world of the flesh. Scholars believe that Jesus' parables constitute the heart of his original and authentic teaching. Put simply, the parables transform the way we look at the world and our lives, challenging our assumptions and opening the door to alternative and countercultural visions of God and our vocation. Like the Zen Buddhist koans, Jesus' parables are intended to break through the prison-house of established knowledge and cultural wisdom, taking us beyond the binary, to experience God's realm springing forth like a mustard seed or seeds planted randomly in a field. They present to us provocative possibilities to help us become emissaries of messy incarnation in our time.

Jesus' parables emerge from real life – farming, unexpected discovery, lost and found, family dynamics, and ethnic prejudice – telling us that God reverses our typical expectations of ethics and goodness. From small beginnings, unnoticed by the powerful and wealthy, a great movement sprouts and bursts forth. A Samaritan outsider manifests heroic compassion. The poor and hungry are invited to a great feast while the wealthy and righteous choose to stay home. An entrepreneur risks everything to acquire a valuable pearl. A billionaire goes to bed delighted at his profits, and cheered by his peers' adulation, only to die during the night. God hears the prayers of the poor and sinful rather than the wealthy and ethical. A widow's coin rings louder in heaven than an entrepreneur's endowment of a Temple building. God is encountered in the least of these and the nations of the world are judged by how they treat the hungry, thirsty, and imprisoned and not by their military strength or economic affluence.

Jesus knew the meaning of the parables first-hand. His whole life was a parable, reflected in his humble birth from an unexpected pregnancy; infancy and childhood in a family without resources fleeing political persecution; the ragtag community of outsiders that composed many of his first followers, and his itinerant life alongside the marginalized. The Word and Wisdom of God manifest in a traveling preacher who colored outside the lines spiritually and ethically and redefined spiritual maturity in terms of hospitality and joy rather than exclusion and legalism. God's Beloved Child accused of being a glutton and partier. Yet, it is in the surprising and unexpected that salvation bursts forth. The light of the world cannot be contained by human institutions, liturgical rights, purity systems, or theological orthodoxies. The parables, in fact, redefine orthodoxy. No longer restricted to right belief, coercively mandated, the orthodox becomes doxological, a call to joyful praise. The ultimate parable, the resurrection, leaves us awestruck as we ponder Jesus' death and our own. The seed bursts forth in the desert, the tomb is empty, a way is made where there is no way.

LIFESTYLE AND POLITICS OF FAITHFULNESS

Jesus embodied his teaching and his teachings inspire us over the centuries. Jesus' approach to life was holistic and relational and so are his teachings in the areas of lifestyle and politics. For Jesus, everything is personal. Everything is also relational, bringing joy and sorrow to our companions and shaping the communities around us. Every act brings greater beauty or ugliness to the world. A simple act can save a soul. A simple touch can liberate energies to heal body, mind, and spirit, and restore persons to their community. When Jesus placed the children on his lap and blessed them, their lives were changed forever. When Jesus let the woman with the jar of perfume anoint him, the two of them were transfigured. When a little boy gave up his lunch, a food-insecure crowd was satisfied. Compassion meted out in daily life has political ramifications, especially when we discover that every action is a gift to God, shaping God's own experience of the world.

Jesus' first message prefigures the rest of his ministry. God's Spirit rests upon and energizes him to:

> bring good news to the poor...
> proclaim release to the captives and recovery of sight to the blind,
> to let the oppressed go free,
> to proclaim the year of God's favor. (Luke 4:18-19)

Life can be a Jubilee, celebrating the beauty of a God-filled world. Jesus' teachings describe the path; the way to live abundantly in a realm embracing, energizing, and enlightening humankind and all creation. From this Jubilee perspective, that is, the vision of spiritual, relational, and economic resources sufficient for all, the collection of sayings known as the Sermon on the Mount can be viewed through the lens of three affirmations, each of which can transform our lives and our communities when embodied in the realities of history:

- You are the light of the world

- God is the Parent (Abba) of us all

- God's realm is incarnate on earth as it is in heaven

The first affirmation, "you are the light of the world," focuses first on Jesus' followers and comes to embrace everyone touched by God's creative wisdom, "the true light which enlightens everyone." (John 1:9) The affirmation of God's universal light is the mantra of the spirit person who experiences God directly and provides a pathway to experiencing God to others. The universality of divine light and revelation reminds us that the sun and the rain fall on the good and bad and friend and foe alike, and challenges us to be "perfect," that is, whole and all-embracing, imitating our "heavenly, all-embracing Parent." Going beyond the binary, we discover blessings and bless others in every condition of life, most especially situations of vulnerability, dependence, and protest. (Matthew 5:3-11) Recognizing something of God in everyone we meet, we discover resources beyond what we can imagine, and as light-bearers, our calling is to bring the light of God to the world, see the light in others, and support their experiences of God's fullness in them.

Light-bearing is personal, interpersonal, and political. Our vocation is to create light-bearing structures and this means challenging, as Jesus did, every economic and political structure that diminishes the light in others. Divine perfection – being perfect as God is perfect - is a call to spiritual and ethical stature. Those who manifest divine perfection are transparent to the moral and spiritual energy of the universe. Opening to God's all-embracing light inspires us to nurture spiritual growth and personal fulfillment in all our human personal and community relationships.

To bear God's light is to embrace God's healing ministry. I have spoken of Jesus' healing ministry and our calling as healing companions in several books.[25] Jesus was a healer, who worked within the patterns of natural causation to elicit the energy of love that heals bodies, minds, spirits, and relationships. A predecessor to today's energy workers, Jesus' energy of love transformed people's cells, relieved pain, calmed their spirits, and awakened the powers of healing enabling them to rise up and walk, be cleansed of skin disease, experience gynecological healing, and awaken from comas. Jesus was a pioneer in what we now describe as holistic or complementary medicine, and his power embodied in prayer, touch, and hospitality still promotes healing and curing in our cellular, spiritual, and relational lives.

The second affirmation, "God is the parent of us all" (paraphrase of Matthew 6:9) orients our spiritual, ethical, relational,

---

25   Bruce Epperly, *God's Touch: Faith, Wholeness, and the Healing Miracles of Jesus* (Westminster/John Knox, 2001); *Healing Worship: Purpose and Practice* (Pilgrim Press, 2006); *Healing Marks: Spirituality and Healing in Mark's Gospel* (Energion, 2012); *Reiki Healing Touch and the Way of Jesus* (Northstone, 2005); *The Energy of Love: Reiki and Christian Healing* (Energion, 2017); *Spirituality and Health, Health and Spirituality* (Twenty-third Publications, 1997).

and political GPS. Taking us beyond divisiveness, we discover that God is the Parent (Abba, Amma) of us all, without exception. Recognizing our divine origins set in motion structures of justice and equality. Those who are God's beloved children – all of us - deserve our respect, affirmation, and just treatment. Ultimately that's what it means us to pray for: God's realm to come "on earth as it is in heaven." Our prayers and actions are intended to incarnate the kin-dom in our world. History is always judged and inspired by the moral and spiritual arcs, the horizons of hope, guiding our behavior forward one moment at a time. While Jesus did not seek to be a political Messiah nor were his followers politically active due to their occupied status and the fact that few initially were Roman citizens and had access to centers of power, the relational and political calling of Jesus' followers is to live by a higher order than political and economic expediency.

This sacramental understanding of life has special meaning for USA citizens. Christians enjoy privileged status and can participate in and influence the political process. Indeed, some Christians are tempted to use their power to persecute others. Living in a democracy, followers of Jesus do not aspire to authoritarian and theocratic power. Living in the way of Jesus inspires the quest for right governance in which our political involvement promotes equality, justice, restoration of past injustice, peacemaking, and welcoming of strangers. This is not an argument for a narrowly Christian political agenda or for Christian exceptionalism. In fact, Christian nationalism and imperialism go against the way of Jesus. However, following the way of Jesus precludes political involvement that promotes racism, separates children from parents at the USA borderlands, dishonesty in political campaigning, and other violent and repressive behaviors.[26]

The Divine Parent embraces all creation. In his counsel to let go of anxiety by seeking God's kin-dom as our ultimate concern, Jesus affirmed that God cares for the birds of the air and the grass

---

26 For more on the role of Christianity in politics, see *Process Theology and Politics* (Gonzales, FL: Energion, 2020).

of the field. The Loving Parent's embrace contains the whole world. The Infinite and Intimate meet in God's love for sparrows, lilies, and little children. Indeed, "God's eye is on the sparrow and I know he's watching us!" Long before the environmental movement, Jesus told us that all life matters – sea life matters, reptile life, land life matters, human life matters, black lives matter. God has the whole world in God's hands.

PROMISE OF THE FUTURE

The kin-dom of God is present and future. God's light shines in all creation, the true light enlightens everyone. (John 1:9) Each of us is the light of the world, the light of Christ, and our essential enlightenment emerges through sacrificial self-awareness. The realm of God is among us and within us, giving us everything we need to bear much fruit. Jesus channeled God's vision of abundant life for all people. (John 10:10) Jesus reminded his followers that we are all branches connected with the divine vine and when we commit ourselves to spiritual practices, God's energy flows through us and we bear great fruit. (John 15:1-11)

The omnipresent God is energetically and creatively present in all creation and each one of us. The non-canonical Gospel of Thomas records Jesus proclaiming:

> I am the light shining upon all things.
> I am the sum of everything,
>   for everything has come forth from me,
> and towards me everything unfolds.
> Split the piece of wood and there I am,
> Pick up a stone and you will find me there. (Logion 77)

In God's kin-dom, there is no "other." As you have done unto the least of these, you have done unto Jesus. (Matthew 25:40). There is no boundary or border in God's love. Beyond the binary, there is a unity that affirms and promotes uniqueness and diversity within the body of Christ (1 Corinthians 12), where social, ethnic, cultural, and sexual diversity is transfigured into creativity and adventure. Again, in the words of the Gnostic Jesus:

> When you are able
> to make the two one,
> the outside like the inside,
> the higher like the lower,
> so that a man is no longer male,
> and a woman, female,
> become a single whole...
> then you may enter in. (Gospel of Thomas, Logion 22)

Unlike certain religious leaders and politicians who hoard power and want to control the future of their ministries, Jesus promoted his followers' success. He wanted them to be interdependent and their interdependence is grounded in and supports personal agency creativity. Human agency is no threat to God. Novelty is no threat to Jesus. Jesus knew that as his followers, the future of the kin-dom is in our hands to be shaped according to our gifts and intentions. We are, as Teresa of Avila asserted, God's hands and feet. God's world is "plus ultra" – much more and constantly growing – rather than "zero-sum" – finite and limited solely to what God can do. God invites our initiative as agents in creating the future for both God and ourselves. In the spirit of Philippians 2:5-11, Jesus leads by letting go of power and creating space for agency. Jesus gives his followers a task – to fish for humans and to share the gospel to every nation, acting on his behalf in our own unique way. While Jesus may not have imagined the institutional church and likely would have been appalled at Constantinian Christendom, whether in the Holy Roman Empire or God and Country American religion, Jesus proclaimed that we had powers beyond our imagination: "the one who believes in me will also do greater works than I do." (John 14:12)

With Socrates, Jesus recognized that "know thyself" is key to embracing God's abundant life. Self-awareness challenges us to grow in wisdom and stature, as Jesus did, and tap into the unlimited reservoirs of divine energy. The realm of God is embodied in the messiness and conflicts of history, slowly emerging like the mustard growing to give life to all creation. The promise of the realm of Shalom lives on for all those who "ask, seek, and knock."

In the messiness of incarnation, when we fallibly embody Jesus' life in our time and place, we will incarnate God's vision of Shalom in the day-to-day tasks of domestic reconciliation, prophetic healing, and world loyalty. We also find Jesus in the temple toppling tables as reflective of his emerging realm of protest and prayer. We will know Jesus in our walking and in the adventures of kin-dom living. We will discover that can we do great things for God and the world. We can be Jesus's companions in saving the earth. That is the promise of Jesus' messy incarnation.

CPSIA information can be obtained
at www.ICGtesting.com
Printed in the USA
LVHW030525161122
733175LV00001B/71